THE WORLD OF
CATS

FACT FINDER

THE WORLD OF CATS

J O A N · M O O R E

CRESCENT BOOKS
New York

A SALAMANDER BOOK

First published by Salamander Books Ltd., 129/137 York Way,
London N7 9LG, United Kingdom.

©Salamander Books Ltd 1989

This 1989 edition published by Crescent Books, distributed by Crown
Publishers, Inc., 225 Park Avenue South, New York, New York 10003.

Printed and bound in Belgium.

ISBN 0-517-69085-3

h g f e d c b a

CREDITS

Editor: Lisa Dyer
American Consultant: Daphne Negus
Designer: Liz Black
Artwork: John Francis
Filmset: The Old Mill, London
Color separation: Scantrans Pte Ltd., Singapore

Printed in Belgium by Proost International Book Production

PICTURE CREDITS

The publishers would like to thank Marc Henrie for supplying the
majority of the photographs in this book. Thanks also go to the
following photographers and agencies. Photographs have been credited
on the page: (B) Bottom, (T) Top, (L) Left.

Ardea: 10, 11(B), 15(T), 16(B), 17(T), 21(T), 44(L), 52(B), 60, 63(B)
Bridgeman Art Library: 9(T)
Bruce Coleman: Front cover (L), 11(T), 22
Mary Evans Picture Library: 8(B), 9(B)
Vicki Jackson: 31, 58(L)
Ronald Sheridan: 8(L)

CONTENTS

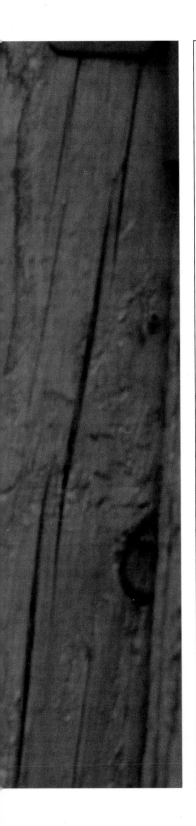

INTRODUCTION TO THE WORLD OF CATS

Surrounded by myth and legend, the cat now enjoys great popularity as more and more people discover just why it is such a fascinating creature. This colourful book is packed with interesting information about the world of cats. For example, did you know that if all the domestic cats in the world were to interbreed they would eventually become tabbies? Every aspect of cats is considered, from practical tips on caring for a cat to the historical and sometimes mythological origins of particular breeds. Part One introduces you to the cat's history, family, anatomy and behaviour. Also included is information for the cat owner on choosing, caring for, grooming and showing a cat. Part Two explains and describes the different breeds of cat, enabling the owner or the admirer to recognize all kinds of pedigree breeds. Whether you already have a cat, are planning to choose one or are simply a lover of cats, this guide will provide you with hours of enjoyable reading.

Left: *This beautiful Sorrel Abyssinian is pictured here in its favourite environment. A great lover of the outdoors, this breed is intelligent, playful and energetic.*

CATS IN HISTORY

Cats were first domesticated in Ancient Egypt as long as 4000 years ago. The Egyptians greatly admired the courage and self-reliance of these beautiful creatures and chose the cat as their symbol of life. Mau, as the Egyptians called the cat, soon became elevated to the status of a god and was known as either Pasht, Bast, Ubastet or Bubastis. As the cat assumed importance in Egypt, so it became a crime to hurt or kill one.

In their mortal existence, cats were treated with the utmost care and affection, sharing meals at the same table as their human family and shown every respect. And, even after death, care was lavished on them. According to their strong religious convictions, the Ancient Egyptians firmly believed in life after death; this was reflected in their treatment of the cat. The remains of a deceased cat were embalmed, adorned with jewelled collars and often artificial ears, wrapped in the finest linen and laid out in ornate mummy cases which were then placed in cat tombs. To provide nourishment for the cat on its journey to the afterworld, mice were also embalmed and placed in the tomb of the cat.

Below: This 17th Century woodcut shows two witches and their cats ('familiars'). In the Middle Ages, cats were persecuted because of their alleged association with witches.

Wall carvings and sculptures unearthed by Egyptologists reveal that the cat of Ancient Egypt was similar in shape and markings to the tabby cat of today. Wall paintings, too, were discovered which showed the cat involved in everyday domestic life.

Thanks to the cat, the Egyptians could raise their crops and store their grain without fear of being over-run by rats, the classic Egyptian plague. As a result, exportation of the cat was forbidden. By about 550 BC, Greeks possessed cats, having stolen them from Egyptians to protect their own harvest. However, there seems to be no evidence that Hebrews or Assyrians kept cats this early.

Cats were known to be in India and China around 500 BC. In the Hindu and Parsee religions, a deep regard for all forms of life meant that the Indians were sympathetic towards the cat and it was considered proper for each Hindu household to own at least one cat. Buddhists throughout Asia revered the quiet, meditative ways of the feline. Some Chinese suspected it of bringing unwelcome poverty to the household but many felt that the cat's ability to see in the dark meant that it could ward off evil spirits.

Around 400 AD, cats were taken from Egypt to Siam (Thailand) by grain merchants, and those cats were probably the ancestors of the Siamese cat we know today. Not

Above: Charms were commonly used in Ancient Egypt; this one shows the Egyptian cat-headed goddess Bastet, found in the tomb of Oudebaounded, circa 1040 BC.

necessarily in the role of pest controller, cats began to appear throughout the Mediterranean regions having been traded as items of curiosity by the Phoenicians during their voyages around that area.

Cats in Britain and America

Tabby cats were known in Britain in 94 AD, since the Welsh king Hywel the Good sold tabby kittens for one penny each — two pennies after a kitten had caught its first mouse! In all probability, the Romans brought the first cats to England. Here, the cat was held in high esteem for its rodent-catching prowess and penalties were introduced for stealing or killing a cat. Domestic cats were a rarity in England at this time. So, with the growing demand for these feline hunters, the cat population increased and vast colonies were soon to be found living in granaries, barns and cellars.

However, as England entered the Middle Ages, with its superstitious fear of witches and the black arts, the cat was no longer the hunter, but the hunted. Previously adored and worshipped, the cat was now thought to be in league with the Devil and it was feared and hated. This hostility continued throughout the Middle Ages and thousands of cats perished. Eventually, with the arrival

Below: *This pen and ink drawing depicts a group of interested visitors at the first British National Cat Show at the Crystal Palace, London, in 1871.*

Above: *The famous cat-lover and artist Louis Wain painted this amusing watercolour 'Afternoon at Home' in 1922.*

of the 18th Century, persecution of the cat decreased and *Felis catus* returned to favour.

Meanwhile, during the 17th Century, cats of the traditional tabby pattern went with the Pilgrim fathers and other early settlers to the Americas — specifically to the Boston area. An interesting fact is that, today, almost half of the cats living in Boston are of this particular tabby pattern and the range which the original venturing toms covered can be determined by cats featuring this coat pattern in the neighbouring areas.

The popularity of the cat increased considerably during Victorian and Edwardian times. The comfortable image of the domestic cat sleeping by the hearth was enhanced by the popular nursery rhymes and children's stories of the day. Around the turn of the century, the artist Louis Wain featured the clever antics of cats dressed in human clothes and striking human attitudes. These adorned postcards, children's books and magazines. Once again, the cat had captured the human heart and imagination.

Today, in the United States of America, the feline is the most popular companion animal. In Britain, too, it is fast becoming the number one pet.

THE CAT FAMILY

Cats first appeared about 12 million years ago and since that time have changed relatively little. There are now many types of cat, both wild and domesticated, and the family name for all cats is Felidae. This family is divided into three groups or genera: *Panthera, Acinonyx,* and *Felis.*

The great roarers, such as the lion, tiger, jaguar and leopard, belong to the *Panthera* group while the cheetah, the only wild cat to have non-retractable claws, belongs to the *Acinonyx* group. The smaller wild cats and the domestic cats are of the *Felis* group. The cat which the Ancient Egyptians regarded so highly and which became the first domesticated cat was almost certainly derived from *Felis lybica,* also called the caffre cat or the African wild cat. Found in Africa,

Asia and certain Mediterranean islands, *F. lybica* is sandy to light brown in colour. *Felis silvestris,* the European wild cat, is *F. lybica's* counterpart in Northern Europe and Asia. It is a greyish coloured cat with black stripes and a black ringed tail.

It is thought that the tabby markings which distinguish the domestic cat are the result of matings between descendants of *lybica* and *silvestris.* Offspring from these matings, however, would be too wild to make suitable pets; while *lybica* can be trained and would breed with the domestic cat, *silvestris* is intolerant of humans, human dwellings and cannot be litter-trained. The domestic cat is similar to *silvestris* only in its ability to produce several litters each year whereas *lybica* produces one.

The Big Cats

Members of this group are the kings of the cat world. Living in the forests and on the savannahs of Africa, Asia and, in the case of the jaguar, America, many of these magnificent creatures are now endangered.

The cheetah, of the genus *Acinonyx,* is the fastest four legged animal at short bursts of speed. It has an extremely fast acceleration rate — from 0 to 64 km/h (0 to 40 mph) in just a few seconds. Over short distances it has been timed at 112 km/h (70 mph) although 80 km/h (50 mph) is more usual.

The Small Cats

Throughout the Felidae family, habits and characteristics remain basically the same. Therefore, by observing members of the

THE BIG CATS

Cheetah *(Acinonyx jubatus)*
Yellow-brown with dark spots. Long legs for high speed. Found throughout Africa, through the Middle East to southern Asia. Weight: 30-50kg (65-110lb).

Clouded leopard *(Panthera nebulosa)*
Pale brown in colour with blotches. Found in southern and south-eastern Asia. Weight: 18-30kg (40-65lb).

Jaguar *(Panthera onca)*
Yellow-brown with spots clustered in rosettes, or dark brown. Found from southern USA to South America. Weight: 40-135kg (90-300lb).

Leopard *(Panthera pardus)*
Pale brown with spots clustered in rosettes, or very dark brown. Found in southern Asia, Indonesia, and most of Africa. Weight: 50-70kg (110-150lb).

Lion *(Panthera leo)*
Sandy brown in colour. The male lion has a mane. Found in Africa, south of the Sahara and, in limited numbers, in India. Weight: 135-225kg (300-500lb).

Snow leopard *(Panthera uncia)*
Light grey with darker rosettes and long haired. Found in central Asia. Weight: 45-70kg (100-155lb).

Tiger *(Panthera tigris)*
Orange-brown with black stripes. The largest and only truly striped cat. Found from southern and south-eastern Asia to north-eastern China and Siberia. Weight: 110-220kg (240-485lb).

Above: *The Siberian Tiger is one of the few cats which will take to water if necessary.*

THE SMALL CATS

African golden cat *(Felis aurata)*
Rich brown to silver grey in colour. Found in Africa. Weight: 13-18kg (28-40lb).

African wild cat *(Felis lybica)*
Light brown with stripes. Probable ancestor of the domestic cat. Found in Africa and Asia, and from the Middle East to India. Also found on some Mediterranean islands. Weight: 4-8kg (9-18lb).

Bay cat *(Felis badia)*
Bright reddish brown in colour. Found in Borneo. Weight: 2-3kg (4-7lb).

Black-footed cat *(Felis nigripes)*
Light brown with dark body markings and black patches under the feet. Found in southern Africa. Weight: 1-2kg (2-4lb).

Bobcat *(Felis rufus)*
Reddish-brown with darker stripes and spots. Found from North America to southern Mexico. Weight: 7-16kg (15-35lb).

Caracal *(Felis caracal)*
Reddish-brown to yellow grey in colour. Tufted ears. Found in Africa, Arabia and northern India. Weight: 16-23kg (35-50lb).

Chinese desert cat *(Felis bieti)*
Yellow-brown in colour with dark broken stripes. Found in Mongolia and China. Weight: 3-6kg (7-13lb).

Domestic cat *(Felis catus, formerly F. domestica)*
A wide range of markings and colourings. Long or short hair. Found throughout the world living in or around human habitation. Sometimes wild or feral. Weight, on average: 3-9kg (7-20lb).

European wild cat *(Felis silvestris)*
Grey tabby cat with black stripes. Black ringed tail with black rounded tip. Found throughout Europe and western Asia. Weight: 4-11kg (9-24lb).

Fishing cat *(Felis viverrina)*
Sandy coloured with dark spots. Slightly webbed paws and claws which are not fully retractable. Found in southern and south-eastern Asia. Weight: 6-8kg (13-18lb).

Flat-headed cat *(Felis planiceps)*
Reddish-brown in colour with a slightly flattened head. Found in south-eastern Asia. Weight: 6-8kg (13-18lb).

Felis group, it is easy to see the relationship between the wild and the domestic cats. The striped tabby coat pattern is prevalent in both wild and domestic cats. A few examples of the rosette blotched tabby coat pattern are also found in both groups. These two coat patterns are often accompanied by agouti hair colouring in which each strand of hair is banded. The band nearest the skin is creamy white, the middle band is yellow, and the band furthest from the skin is a black 'tipping'. This agouti hair colouring can be found in rabbits, cavies, squirrels and mice as well as in some domestic cats.

The domestic cat is the smallest of the *Felis* group and is distinguished from other members by its wide range of markings and colours and variation of hair length — it may be either long or shorthaired.

Right: *The African wild cat (Felis lybica) is an ancestor of the modern domestic cat.*

Geoffroy's cat *(Felis geoffroyi)*
Grey or sandy with dark spots. Found from Bolivia to Patagonia in South America. Weight: 2-5kg (4-11lb).

Iriomote cat *(Felis iriomtensis)*
Sandy coloured with dark spots. Discovered in 1964. Similar to the leopard cat. Found on the island of Iriomote, near Taiwan. Weight: 5-6kg (11-13lb).

Jaguarundi *(Felis yagouaroundi)*
Grey-brown or brownish-red in colour. Found in Central and South America. Weight: 5-10kg (11-22lb).

Jungle cat *(Felis chaus)*
Sandy-brown with some markings and a ringed tail. Found in Egypt and southern Asia. Weight: 7-14kg (15-30lb).

Kodkod *(Felis guigna)*
Grey with dark spots and ringed tail. Found in South America. Weight: 2-3kg (4-7lb).

Leopard cat *(Felis bengalensis)*
Varying coat colour with dark spots. Found in south-eastern Asia, from India to the Philippines, Japan, Manchuria and eastern Siberia. Weight: 3-7kg (7-15lb).

Lynx *(Felis lynx)*
Light brown with dark spots and tufted ears. Found in Europe, northern Asia and North America. Weight: 14-29kg (30-64lb).

Marbled cat *(Felis marmorata)*
Light brown with a marbled pattern of dark blotches. Found in south-eastern Asia. Weight: 5-7kg (11-15lb).

Margay *(Felis wiedii)*
Yellow-brown with dark spots and stripes. Ringed tail. Found in Central and South America. Weight: 4-8kg (9-18lb).

Mountain cat *(Felis jacobita)*
Brown to grey in colour with dark spots and a ringed tail. Found in South America. Weight: 3-7kg (7-15lb).

Ocelot *(Felis pardalis)*
Yellow or grey with dark spots and stripes and a ringed tail. Found from southern USA to South America. Weight: 5-13kg (11-28lb).

Below: *The Margay is known as an arborea (tree-climbing) species.*

Pallas's cat *(Felis manul)*
Orange-grey in colour. Black and white head markings. Found in central Asia. Weight: 3-5kg (7-11lb).

Pampas cat *(Felis colocolo)*
Grey with dark spots. Found in South America. Weight: 3-7kg (7-15lb).

Puma *(Felis concolor)*
Sandy to black in colour. Largest of the small cats. Also known as mountain lion, cougar and panther. Found in North, Central and South America. Weight: 45-60kg (100-130lb).

Rusty-spotted cat *(Felis rubiginosa)*
Dark red coloured with brown blotches. Found in southern India and Sri Lanka. Weight: 1-2kg (2-4lb).

Sand cat *(Felis margarita)*
Yellow-brown to grey-brown with ringed tail. Hair over the paw pads. Found in northern Africa, the Middle East and south-western Asia. Weight: 2-3kg (4-7lb).

Serval *(Felis serval)*
Sandy with dark spots. Slender build with large ears, long legs and a short tail. Found in Africa. Weight: 13-18kg (28-40lb).

Temminck's golden cat *(Felis temmincki)*
Golden brown with black face markings. Found in Tibet and south-western China. Weight: 6-11kg (13-24lb).

Tiger cat *(Felis tigrina)*
Sandy in colour with dark stripes and blotches. Found in Central and South America. Weight: 2-5kg (4-11lb).

THE CAT'S BODY

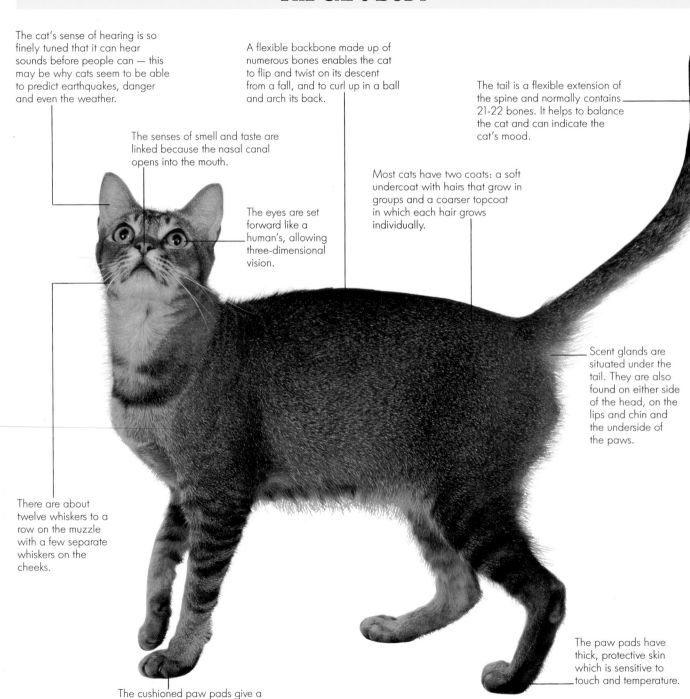

The cat's sense of hearing is so finely tuned that it can hear sounds before people can — this may be why cats seem to be able to predict earthquakes, danger and even the weather.

A flexible backbone made up of numerous bones enables the cat to flip and twist on its descent from a fall, and to curl up in a ball and arch its back.

The tail is a flexible extension of the spine and normally contains 21-22 bones. It helps to balance the cat and can indicate the cat's mood.

The senses of smell and taste are linked because the nasal canal opens into the mouth.

The eyes are set forward like a human's, allowing three-dimensional vision.

Most cats have two coats: a soft undercoat with hairs that grow in groups and a coarser topcoat in which each hair grows individually.

Scent glands are situated under the tail. They are also found on either side of the head, on the lips and chin and the underside of the paws.

There are about twelve whiskers to a row on the muzzle with a few separate whiskers on the cheeks.

The paw pads have thick, protective skin which is sensitive to touch and temperature.

The cushioned paw pads give a cat its softly padding gait.

It has been said that the cat's body is a superb hunting machine. Certainly it is lithe and muscular and can run, leap and climb swiftly and with precision. Cats are surefooted with a good sense of balance and have highly sensitive sensory organs which are always on the alert. They use their claws and strong hind legs to climb trees and can jump from reasonable heights gracefully and with comparative ease, landing on all four feet. It is untrue to say that cats, anymore than other animals, can leap from great heights without hurting themselves.

The Ears

Cat's ears are extremely sensitive and can hear sounds more highly pitched than we can. They can turn independently to face the direction of sound and will also express the cat's moods, such as fear, aggression or contentment. An arrangement of small muscles situated in the ears can reduce vibrations caused by loud sounds. The ear mechanisms are so delicate, they can often become damaged. Consequently, many older cats are deaf. Sight and smell then become more keen to compensate for the lack of hearing.

THE CAT'S EYES

The pupil of the cat's eye becomes open and round in darkness to allow more light rays to enter.

The pupil narrows to a slit in bright daylight to shut out some of the sun's rays.

This thin membrane, called a haw, often appears in illness. It helps lubricate and protect the cornea.

The Eyes

Cats have excellent vision in daylight, but, contrary to popular opinion, they do not see perfectly well in the dark. They do, however, have a unique tissue at the back of the eye called *tapetum lucidium,* which enables them to make the most of very dim light. At night, the pupil of a cat's eye opens in order to catch as much light as possible. In a bright light, such as sunlight, the pupil narrows to a mere slit. When a cat is unwell, a third eyelid — the nictitating membrane or 'haw' — appears. This is a greyish membrane which extends from the inside of the eye, helping to protect and moisten it. The cat has a remarkable range of eye colour — from copper, gold, orange and a variety of greens to various shades of blue.

The Nose

The nose and paw pads are two hairless areas on the cat's body. Both are protected by skin 75 times thicker than that covering other areas and each has an individual design, like a human fingerprint. The nose is extremely sensitive to temperature and pressure. The cat's sense of smell is closely linked with the sense of taste and the cat may be seen smelling its food 'disdainfully' prior to tasting it! In an unfamiliar place a cat will smell out its surroundings, perhaps catching the scent left by an earlier cat. A keen sense of smell is particularly necessary to the cat in the wild, whose survival depends on its ability to sniff out the scent of its prey.

The Mouth and Jaws

The cat is a carnivore (a meat-eater) and, reflecting this, its jaws are designed for efficiently killing, tearing and devouring prey. Though not entirely dependent on prey for its survival, the domestic cat, with its strong hinged jaws, sharp canine or 'killing' teeth, and carnassials or 'tearing' teeth, is not far removed from the cat in the wild. The adult cat has thirty teeth including four canines — the latter usually being through by the time a kitten is seven months old. Saliva, which in the human is used to start the digestion process, is, in the cat, an aid in helping the food down the throat. Powerful digestive juices in the stomach and small intestine help break down the food. The cat's tongue is flexible and muscular. The surface of the tongue is rough and bears special sensory detectors which assess temperature and taste. The tongue's roughness is caused by tiny 'knobs' called papillae which, during grooming, act like a comb on the cat's fur.

UNSHEATHING THE CLAWS

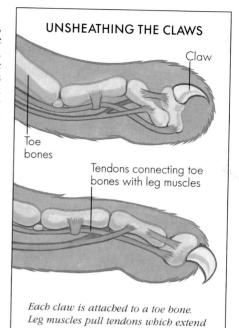

Each claw is attached to a toe bone. Leg muscles pull tendons which extend the toe and claw outwards.

The Whiskers

The whiskers, or vibrissae, are believed to act as antennae or feelers, helping a cat to judge the widths through which its body passes. Whiskers are also extremely expressive, indicating when a cat is annoyed, frightened or even inquisitive.

The Paws and Claws

A cat's paw is a complex structure. The forepaw has five toe pads, five claws and two large pads. The fifth claw acts like a human thumb and is used in climbing and holding on to prey. The hind paw has four toe pads, four claws and one large pad. The paw is used when climbing, feeding, washing, digging, hunting and playing.

The paw pad is also used to 'scent mark' boundaries such as trees and fences. The claws are curved, sharp and, with minor exceptions, sheathed when not in use.

The Tail

The tail is a flexible extension of the spine and the cat uses this in many ways: to maintain balance, to steer while swimming and in the expression of moods. It is also often used as a teaching aid by the mother cat. For instance, to encourage the hunting skills of her kittens, the mother allows them to stalk and pounce on her own tail.

CAT BEHAVIOUR

Throughout the cat world, behaviour patterns remain basically the same. Significant displays of behaviour can be a method of communication — not only to the cat's own kind but also to the humans with whom it has contact. From the earliest cat, thousands of years ago, these unique displays have been able to indicate to others the cat's moods, its territory markings or its mating rituals. Some behaviour patterns are instinctive or inborn, such as hunting and the maternal instinct. Others, like toilet-training, are taught to the kitten by its mother.

Hunting

Hunting is a way of life for the cat in the wild, and, to a lesser degree, this is also the case with the domestic cat. Wild or domesticated, the instincts of the cat are basically the same: the movement of the prey provides the cat with the stimulus to attack and, according to the behaviour of the prey, the cat's capturing techniques vary. In the wild, the swift cheetah chases its prey, often to the point of exhaustion. Smaller cats generally sever the spinal cord of their prey with their canine teeth. Larger cats, such as the lion, jump on to the haunches of their prey and break the animal's back. Tigers will usually attack the throat. The domestic cat belongs to the smaller cat category and, as it does not need to kill to eat, will often toy with its prey and may carry it around in its mouth without actually killing it.

Below: A cat's expression will often reveal its moods, feelings and intentions!

Sexual Behaviour

A very important part of instinctive cat behaviour is related to the mating ritual. As the female comes into season or is 'on heat', her behaviour changes quite dramatically. She becomes very affectionate, often rubbing herself against her owner's legs and, as she approaches her most fertile period, increasingly displays her hind quarters beneath a lifted tail. The un-spayed female cat may become frustrated if she is denied access to a male cat. She 'calls', often loudly, and emits subtle body scents which are recognized by the un-neutered (entire or unaltered) male cat. This, in turn, causes him to begin mating.

When the mating act is complete, the female turns on the male in an aggressive manner whereupon he leaps to safety — usually to a high vantage point.

Territory Marking

Cats are particularly 'territorial' animals and territory marking is a part of instinctive behaviour. There are several ways in which a cat marks its territory and each one indicates the route a cat has taken, its sex and its status. The most effective method is urine spraying gateposts, trees and corners, which are then pungently marked. An alternative method is scratching or pawing territory boundaries. This way, the scent from the paw pads is left for others to smell. Depositing scent from glands behind the ears and at the root of the tail is done by rubbing the head and entwining the tail on and around the boundaries. People may also represent these boundaries and a cat may often be seen rubbing its head against the face of its own special person (usually its owner's face), or even entwining its body and tail around that person's legs.

Maternal Behaviour

The maternal behaviour which a mother cat displays to her offspring ensures that the kitten is cared for and taught all the essential behaviour patterns necessary to the adult cat. The female cat makes a very attentive mother and the bond between mother and kitten will continue through to that kitten's adulthood, providing there is no break in the relationship. Mother cat, from the moment of her kittens' birth, will busy herself clean-

Below: 'Play-fighting' is one of the many feline behavioural patterns. A kitten's 'play' development will echo early hunting instincts. Even older 'kittens', like those pictured here, enjoy the game!

A contented cat has alert ears, relaxed whiskers and well-adjusted eyes.

A blissful cat has relaxed ears and half-closed eyes. It will probably be purring!

A frightened cat flattens its ears and whiskers. The eyes are wide and the fur bristled.

An aggressive cat's eyes will be slitted and its teeth bared.

ing up the little ones, drawing them close to her warm body and stimulating their mouths for their first feed. She will nurse, protect and guard her kittens for long periods of time, leaving the nest only briefly for her own food and drink.

Over the following weeks the mother will teach her kittens all there is to know about being a cat. When their eyes open after about eight to ten days, she will begin to litter train her young. After feeding, she will take each kitten in her mouth, place it in the litter tray, and encourage urination and defecation by using her rough tongue under the tiny tail to stimulate bowel movement. She will then show the kitten how to cover the waste matter by using her front paws. As the kittens grow, the mother cat will move them to a new site to accommodate their increasing activity and to ensure minimum danger. The widening range of natural behaviour patterns displayed by kittens includes play-fighting between litter-mates and the hunting sequence — stalking, pouncing and pawing a dangling toy which, at this stage, is as interesting as any mouse!

Grooming

Grooming, either of itself or of cat companions, is an important part of feline behaviour and time devoted to this can take up to one-third of a cat's waking hours. In addition to keeping its fur smooth and clean by removing dead hair and skin cells, grooming can also regulate the cat's temperature. A cat can often be seen grooming itself in moments of indecision or fright.

When cats groom each other this is called 'social grooming' — giving great pleasure to the cats and often accompanied by much purring! Grooming sessions also reinforce the bond between mother and kitten.

Right: Cats spend long periods totally absorbed in self-grooming. This usually occurs after eating but also when otherwise unoccupied. Pictured here, a lovely Somali is paying particular attention to its paws.

Below: Showing a colourful assortment of coats, a contented Tortoiseshell mother cat relaxes with her young. She gives them close supervision and security while they rest.

CHOOSING YOUR CAT

What type of cat is best for you? Do you want a kitten or a cat, a pedigree or non-pedigree, a male or female, a longhair or shorthair? And, are you prepared to spend time training, grooming and caring for a cat? There are also other factors to consider, such as: are there members of your family who are allergic or even frightened of cats? All these questions *must* be considered carefully before purchasing your new pet. A kitten grows into a cat and could be with you for twelve to fifteen years or more, so your decision must be the right one.

Kitten or Cat
Like all young things, kittens are playful, often boisterous and need to be trained. If there are elderly people in your home, a kitten may well get under their feet and if there is a young child, it may not realize the danger of sharp little claws. And if no one is at home during the day, a kitten, missing the protective warmth of its mother, could be lonely and unhappy.

If you feel able to take on the responsibility of a kitten, which means feeding at least four times a day up to eight months old, being patient with regard to litter training and being prepared to clean up the small mistakes that sometimes happen, then a kitten is for you. On the other hand, buying an adult cat has many advantages.

Adult cats are much quieter than kittens. They are independent, somewhat set in their ways and will sit quietly, out of mischief. They do not need to be kept occupied as much as a kitten. An adult cat will almost certainly be litter trained and will not require constant supervision in the home. It will also sleep for fairly long periods of time — probably on your bed!

Buying Non-pedigree Cats
Local farms or rescue organizations are often a good source for acquiring non-pedigrees, and sometimes a cat breeder whose queen (breeding female) has mismated, has half-pedigree kittens for sale. If possible, try to see the kitten with its mother and litter-mates before making the final choice — by looking at the mother you will get a good idea what your kitten may eventually look like.

Make sure that the kitten's eyes and nose are not sticky nor its ears dirty, and that its tail is clean and dry. The stomach should

Above: The two non-pedigree cats pictured here are keeping themselves warm by curling up together. Cats can enjoy each other in a quiet way as well as in active games.

not be swollen. Also ensure that it is fully inoculated before taking it home. Rescue organizations often have adult cats ready to go to good homes. These cats are usually clean and fully inoculated. All desperately need to be loved and cared for.

Buying Pedigree Cats
Buy pedigree cats from a reputable breeder. When selecting, the above guidelines also apply and when taking your chosen pedigree kitten home do not forget the following: the kitten's pedigree certificate, registration certificate, a suitable diet sheet and, if available, a list of the basic dos and don'ts of rearing a kitten of your chosen breed. If in any doubt during the first few weeks of looking after your kitten, contact the breeder for advice. Books on caring for breeds are also obtainable at your local library.

Below: Whether you are bringing your cat home for the first time or taking it to the vet or to a show, the safest way for it to travel is inside a special carrying case.

Welcome Home

Before you leave to collect your cat or kitten, make sure you have everything ready for its arrival in its new home. Some necessary items include: a medium size, draught-proof box or basket; food and water dishes; cat or kitten food; litter tray and litter; paper towels; a small warm blanket; and toys such as a lightweight ball, or a furry mouse.

Place the paper towels at the bottom of the box or basket and make a firm nest out of the blanket. Once everything is ready, collect your new friend, taking with you a special carrying basket or cardboard pet container. If you have a kitten, remember that taking it from its mother is a big step. It is quite natural that it will feel cold and lonely. Leave food, water and the litter tray within easy reach, but place the latter away from the food as cats prefer to use their tray some distance away from their eating area. After the kitten's arrival, try to make allowances for its use of the litter tray. If the kitten is doubtful about what to do, lift it into the litter tray after eating. The adult cat should be aware of what to do but, in a strange environment, it may need reminding at first.

After a short period of adjustment, your cat or kitten will come to regard you and your family as its own. A harmonious relationship is essential for the wellbeing of all concerned so cherish and love your cat and it will respond with affection and loyalty.

Above: *Two cats will keep each other occupied by playing together while a single cat, if isolated, may become bored.*

Left: *It is not easy to identify the sex of a kitten; here, male and female are shown.*

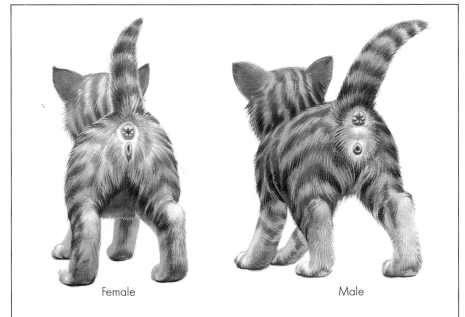

Female   Male

YOUR NEW KITTEN

- Make sure your chosen kitten's appearance is fresh and its actions bright and lively.

- Put a comforting well-protected hot water bottle in your kitten's bed.

- Make time to play with your kitten so it does not feel lonely.

- Do not startle your kitten with loud and abrupt noises.

CARING FOR YOUR CAT

To strengthen the special bond between owner and cat, the owner must be fully aware of the cat's special needs and requirements. These quite basic necessities include food, warmth, security and a loving, caring relationship. Always make sure that there is a comfortable, draught-proof box for your cat to sleep in, food and water for when it is hungry or thirsty and a clean litter tray within easy reach. Cats often sleep when they are on their own but remember when leaving your cat the basic necessities to include a favourite toy. Cats often get bored and their choice of 'toy' — such as wire or string — can be unsuitable or even dangerous. There are also many other ways in which you can ensure the comfort and contentment of your feline friend.

Regular Meals

Regular, nourishing meals should be provided for your cat or kitten. Unlike its cousin in the wild, your cat does not have to hunt for its food. Therefore, it is up to you to provide food which covers all the cat's dietary needs — many pet food manufacturers supply diet sheets for cats of all ages. If your cat were to hunt for mice, these little creatures would supply a useful cross-section of natural nutrients. However, your cat still would not receive its correct quota and, in any case, the consumption of mice is not recommended for today's household pet due to probable worm infestation.

Whenever possible, keep to your cat's 'biological clock'. Routine will give your cat a strong sense of security which will help to

Above: Pictured here, a special relationship of affection and companionship is exhibited by a young girl and her cat.

make it a contented, confident cat. The adult cat may be fed two or three times a day. A kitten of up to eight weeks, on the other hand, requires four or five small meals each day because its stomach is only the size of a walnut and cannot digest much at any one time. When serving your kitten's food, keep that 'walnut size' in mind to avoid bouts of colic and indigestion. Many people complain that their cat likes only certain types of food, so don't fall into the habit of feeding a kitten the food that it thinks it likes best. From the first, choose the kind of food that is convenient for you and your cat will adapt to it. Also bear in mind that a healthy cat never looks fat — so do not overfeed.

Worming

Whether or not your cat is a hunter of rodents and birds, it should be wormed on a regular basis. If worms are detectable, ask your vet's advice on how to eradicate them. The vet will be able to supply the correct medication according to the infestation.

Neutering

It is in the best interests of your cat, yourself and your neighbours if he is neutered or she is spayed. Without the powerful urge to procreate, your cat will be a much more docile creature to handle. There will be no more spraying by the male and no more 'calling' or destructive behaviour displayed by the female when in season.

The decision to neuter must be made early. Male cats neutered after they have reached adulthood may retain the habits of the un-neutered (entire) male and continue to spray. Ask your vet's advice on when is the best time to neuter or spay your kitten.

Safety

Take all sensible precautions to keep your cat or kitten as safe and secure as possible. Never let your cat wander so that it is at danger from the traffic and certainly never allow it out at dusk or nightfall. This is a time when your cat will be at grave risk from cat-thieves, cat-fights, traffic and the elements.

There are so many dangers awaiting the wandering cat and the alternative of keeping it either indoors or in a safe garden or backyard eliminates the worry. Creating an escape-proof garden is a very good idea but can be difficult to do since most cats are great climbers. Your cat or kitten will not then be underfoot indoors and it can play outside while under supervision.

If you cannot create such an environment, many cats can be trained to wear harness and lead so they may be taken for walks. It is easiest, however, to train a young adult of around nine to ten months old to this method of exercise. Cats are more difficult than dogs to train and training periods should last, at most, only five minutes at a time. Longer than this and your cat could become bored, fretful and reluctant to lead-train altogether.

Right: *There is a special way to hold a cat or kitten. Support the cat firmly but gently with both hands.*

Holding Your Cat

So that your cat feels secure when being handled, it is important that you support the cat correctly. Hold your cat close to your body and, with one hand under the chest, support its weight with your other hand. *Never* pick up your cat or kitten by the scruff of the neck — this could cause serious injury. Kittens in particular are very fragile and must be handled gently. If your cat struggles, this means that it is uncomfortable and must be freed from your arms. This especially applies to the adult cat who could scratch you quite badly if it objects to being held.

Other Household Pets

When introduced to each other at kitten and puppy stage, contrary to myth, cats and dogs can live quite happily together. Be aware that small pets such as birds, mice and fish may be at risk from your cat. A cat cannot be blamed for doing what comes naturally, so keep other small pets away from it.

Above: *Make sure that you know where your cat is at all times. It could be playing on the road which is dangerous for the cat itself and may result in traffic accidents.*

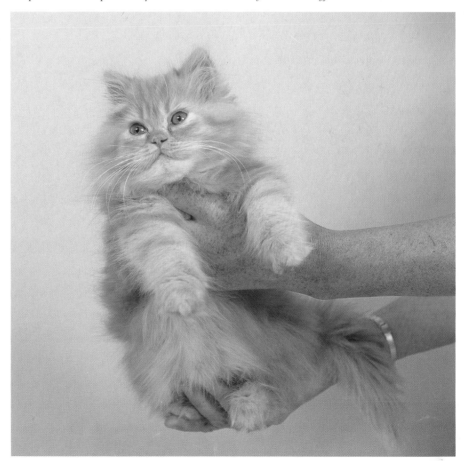

Although self-grooming does take place, the cat's owners should also do their part. Grooming not only maintains the health and cleanliness of the cat, but also strengthens the friendship between cat and owner.

If yours is a shorthaired cat, then grooming three times a week is sufficient. With a longhaired cat, it is essential that you groom it each day. A ten minute routine should prevent unsightly, unhealthy matting of the hair which, if left for too long, may require veterinary attention. Suggested grooming equipment includes a soft brush, a metal comb with easy-to-hold handle, a double-sided flea comb — one side with wider teeth than the other, flea powder, and cotton wool swabs (cotton balls).

Grooming Shorthaired Cats
First, using the metal comb, comb away from the head towards the tail. Remove any loose hair by brushing gently but firmly with the soft brush. Many people 'hand-groom' shorthaired cats by running the palm of the hand quite firmly from head to tail. This 'polishes' the coat and gives it a good shine.

Grooming Longhaired Cats
Follow instructions as for the shorthaired cat, but comb gently, holding each portion of hair as you comb, to avoid causing discomfort. Then give a final brushing with the soft brush.

Fleas
The grooming session may reveal signs of fleas. These must be eliminated for the health and comfort of both your cat and your family. Fleas breed quickly, so don't delay — use a reputable flea powder or spray. Ask someone to help you apply the medication as your cat may take strong and violent exception to this exercise!

Eyes and Ears
Soak a cotton wool swab (cotton ball) in sterile, tepid water and gently clean the eye, working from the outside to inside, nearest the nose. Use a fresh swab if debris is not completely removed. To avoid infection being passed from one eye to the other, use a fresh swab for each eye.

If the inside of the ear is dirty, wipe gently with a swab dampened with baby oil, then dry with another cotton wool swab. Do not

Above: This young cat-owner is busy grooming her cat. Grooming requires special care, time and effort but the result of a beautiful and healthy cat is worthwhile.

poke further into your cat's ears as this may cause permanent damage to its delicate and sensitive hearing mechanisms.

Mouth
Occasionally check inside your cat's mouth for sore gums or tartar on the teeth. Tartar is a brown, scaly substance often found at the edge of gums and teeth. It must be removed by your vet to avoid gum infection.

Claws
Access to concrete floors or a scratching board or post will keep your cat's claws neat and trim. Trimming the claws is rarely necessary and then only by an experienced adult or veterinarian using the correct type of clippers.

Bathing
Bathing your cat should be unnecessary unless it is especially dirty or needs to be well-groomed for a show. If you do need to bath your cat, a mild soap for babies or a 'special pet' shampoo is recommended, followed by brisk and thorough drying.

SHOWING YOUR CAT

Showing your cat can be great fun — especially if it wins a rosette and prize. And even if your cat does not win, the preparation and seeing all the other cats in their pens can still be an exciting experience!

There are many types of show in which you may enter your cat, from the local pet shows in the village hall to the large 'area' shows which usually take place at a leisure centre or exhibition hall. Both pedigree and non-pedigrees may be shown, but if your cat is a non-pedigree, it may be entered in the 'Household Pet' classes only.

Breed shows are a different matter. These deal with cats of one particular breed and only pedigree cats of that breed may be entered in this type of show.

Showing a pedigree cat can be a complicated procedure for the young person so it is recommended that this should be done under the guidance of an adult — especially as showing cats often involves travelling some distance to a show.

Preparation for the Show
There are a number of items to take to the show. These usually include: a white blanket; white dishes for food and water (a wide-based double compartment dish is best as this is not easily tipped over); a white litter tray and litter — although many shows do provide litter for the cats; and a soft brush to give your cat a final groom.

The United States of America is one country which allows a wide range of colours and decorations in competitions. It is best to contact your cat association on the formalities.

Many cats have a nervous disposition. If this is the case with your cat, it would be unwise and unkind to keep your cat in a pen for up to eight hours to be stared at by large crowds of people. So, if you want to show your cat, make sure that it is happy being with people. Also, try to introduce it to 'show business' as early as possible — three or four months old is the earliest.

Above: This prize-winning Perisan looks proud of its well-deserved rosettes. Winning a competition requires, most importantly, care and effort on behalf of the owner.

Non-pedigree Classes
There are many types of classes in the Household Pet section of a show. These are often for the cat with the most expressive eyes, the shiniest coat, or the most appealing face, which makes this section a very interesting one.

Showing Pedigree Cats
There are two governing bodies in the British cat fancy: The Governing Council of the Cat Fancy (GCCF) and the Cat Association (CA). Each has its own method of judging. The GCCF judge cats at their pens and to a closed hall where the public is prohibited. The CA subscribes to 'ring judging', as does the Cat Fanciers Association (CFA) in America, the Canadian Cat Association (CCA), and various bodies in Europe. A relatively new cat association in America is The International Cat Association (TICA). In 'ring judging', the cat is judged before interested onlookers and comments are offered to the owner. Information regarding shows may be obtained from any of these organizations.

Left: Ring judging is an informal way to judge a cat and comments from the judge can often be helpful to the cat-owner — especially if the owner is a newcomer.

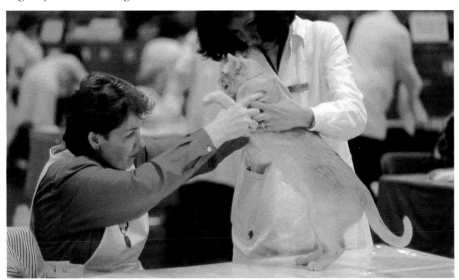

PART TWO

INTERNATIONAL BREEDS OF CAT

Generally, pedigree cats are 'true bred' cats, mated only with members of their own breed. A breed can have several varieties — as in the Siamese (and its derivitives called the Colourpoint Shorthairs in the United States) which shows a wide range of colours and coat patterns. Some breeds occur naturally, that is to say, they evolve by themselves and their colour and coat type are often influenced by their original environment. One example of a naturally occuring breed is the Abyssinian with its 'ticked' rabbit-like coat which offered suitable camouflage in its native scrubland. On the other hand, many cat breeds are 'man-made' by mating various cats to produce a desired type. One of these is the Oriental Spotted Tabby whose breeder, intrigued by the ancient Egyptian Mau, 're-created' this lovely cat by cross-breeding foreign type cats which had similarities to the original Mau. All the different breeds have intriguing and unusual beginnings and unique qualities — as you will discover on the following pages.

__Left:__ Here, the gentle Russian Blue is seen against a flowery background. Its distinctive blue coat, tipped with silver, shimmers in the sunlight.

SHORTHAIRED CATS

Until the end of the 16th Century, the only types of cat known in Europe were shorthaired. These cats were usually of the tabby coat pattern and looked very similar to their ancestor, *Felis lybica*.

The Shorthair pedigrees were originally bred from non-pedigree working mouser cats which suffered the rigours of harsh weather with little domestic comfort. As a result, today's Shorthair has a solid physique and hardy adaptability. These assets, along with a placid nature and an easy-care coat, make the Shorthair an ideal domestic pet.

There are many different breeds of Shorthair with a wide range of colours and coat patterns. The British Shorthair has a stocky, short build described as 'cobby'. The Continental equivalent of the British Shorthair

is known as the European Shorthair. Both are similar in appearance and usually judged by similar breed standards.

By contrast, the American Shorthair has a different breed standard from the British Shorthair. The standard requires a more lightly built cat with a less cobby face and longer ears. The American cat is also slightly longer in the leg and tail than the British variety. Other breeds in this section include the American Wirehair, a mutation of the American Shorthair, and the Exotic Shorthair, a hybrid breed.

Below: This odd-eyed White is a typical example of the cobby British Shorthair. Its velvety white coat and different coloured eyes make it a strikingly distinctive cat.

THE BRITISH SHORTHAIR

The British Shorthair is one of the most popular breeds of cat today. It has a gentle, placid nature and is very affectionate and highly intelligent. This cat has a sturdy, compact body, short strong legs, rounded paws and a thick tail. Its head is massive and round and the eyes are round. One of this cat's distinctive features is its thick, dense coat.

The British Shorthair has many colours and coat patterns. Among these are solid colours such as white, black, blue, red and cream, and combinations of colours as found in the bi-colour, smoke, tabby, tortoiseshell and tipped coat pattern. Regardless of colour or coat pattern, all British Shorthairs have the same general body build and are selectively bred to maintain the deep-chested cobby look.

The Black British Shorthair
The Black British Shorthair originated from the non-pedigree domestic shorthaired cat in the late 19th Century. Its coat should be short, dense and solid black with no sign of single white hairs or 'rustiness' caused by exposure to strong sunlight.

Black cats are often 'melanistic' which means that their black colouring covers a tabby coat pattern — as in the black panther which displays leopard's spots when seen in a certain light. The black panther is often referred to as a 'melanistic leopard'. In the same way, faint tabby pattern markings are sometimes discernable in the coat of self or solid coloured black cats. In the adult Black Shorthair this would be considered a fault on the show bench. However, a melanistic coat can often be seen in kittens and, up to the time kittens are six months old, will be accepted in shows.

The adult Black British Shorthair should have a medium to large, muscular body with a level back and strong short legs as well as a broad, round head on a short neck. The nose should be straight, broad and short and the small, rounded ears set well apart. The cat's nose leather and paw pads should be black and the eyes copper or orange.

The White British Shorthair
It is strange to note that the pure white cat, (except in albinoism which is an abnormality) is rare, despite the fact that white is the most dominant of all coat colours. This is probably because nature determines that a white cat, in the wild, would be too conspicuous — a major disadvantage to a hunter

such as the cat. However, white patching in the non-pedigree is very common.

In long and shorthaired pedigree cats there are three varieties of white cat: the blue-eyed White, the odd-eyed White (one eye orange and the other blue), and the orange-eyed White. Pure white cats with blue eyes are often found to be deaf — this deafness may affect either one or both ears. To produce a White Shorthair with hearing, cat breeders mated blue-eyed Whites with orange-eyed Whites. This resulted in cats

with odd-coloured eyes. These odd-eyed Whites are not usually deaf. Kittens with all three eye colours may be born in a litter.

Coat colour in the White Shorthair should be pure white. Blue-eyed kittens with other colours in their ancestry may have a faint patch of colour on their heads. If this remains, the kitten may be able to hear. The nose leather and paw pads must be pink but, as these cats are genetically white (the colour is inherited from their parents) and not albino, no pink must show in the eyes.

Illustrated here, the Black and White British Shorthairs show their compact build and glossy coat. These self coloured cats have a purity of colour, solid from the roots of their fur to the tips.

Black British
Shorthair

Odd-eyed White
British Shorthair

The Cream British Shorthair

Perfect colouring of the Cream Shorthair is difficult to achieve. As a result, a good example of this breed is very rare.

Ideally, the Cream should have an even-coloured coat of pale cream with no visible tabby markings. Since cream is a dilute (a paler version) of red, it is difficult to produce a coat that is not too reddish ('hot') in colour. If the coat standard is achieved, the Cream is a unique and lovely cat. The cat's nose leather and paw pads should be pink and the eyes a rich copper or orange.

The Blue British Shorthair

This cat is also known as the British Blue and was one of the first breeds to be shown in Britain. The Blue is probably the most popular and has the most gentle nature of all the British Shorthairs.

The Blue has dense, medium to light blue fur which is extremely plush (but firm to the touch in US competition). Describing a cat's coat colour as 'blue' does not mean a sky blue but a medium grey-blue. The cat's nose leather and paw pads should be blue, and the eyes a brilliant copper or orange.

The Blue is almost identical in type to the Chartreux from France. In Britain, the Chartreux is judged by the same standards as the British Blue. It has the same strong body of the British Shorthair but varies slightly by having a less rounded head and a more silvery coat. In the USA, the Chartreux is judged as a separate breed and the colour of the coat varies from ash to slate.

FACT FILE

- Dark slate blue was the ideal colour for the British Blue in the late 1800s but today's standard is for light to medium blue.

- In North America, some cat associations group bi-colours and tortoiseshell patterns under the name Parti-colours.

- The Tortie and White is known as the Calico because it resembles multi-coloured calico fabric.

- The Chartreux from France was allegedly bred by Carthusian monks.

The Bi-colour British Shorthair

The Bi-colour British Shorthair has a white coat which is patched with evenly distributed areas of a second colour in black, blue, red or, more rarely, cream.

The cat's feet, legs, underparts and muzzle should be white with no coloured hairs and patches should show no tabby markings. A blaze of white from forehead to nose is desirable. The nose leather and paw pads should be pink or correspond to the main patched colour. The eyes should be brilliant copper or orange.

The British Tipped Shorthair

The British Tipped Shorthair has an underlying white coat but the very ends or 'tips' of the hair are another colour. This cat is the shorthaired version of the longhaired Chinchilla or Cameo Persian (see page 38). The tipping can occur in the following colours: black, blue, chocolate, lilac, red or cream. The nose leather and paw pads of the Tipped should be pink or match the tipping. The eyes should be copper or orange rimmed in deep rose or, in the Black Tipped, green with black rims.

As seen here, the British Shorthair has many varieties of colour and coat pattern.

Red and White Bi-colour British Shorthair

Blue British Shorthair

Tipped British Shorthair (Chinchilla)

Cream British Shorthair

The Tortoiseshell British Shorthair

The Tortoiseshell or Tortie is a mainly female breed with the occasional sterile male. The coat should be black and evenly patched with red and cream. A red or cream blaze on the head is particularly desirable at the UK show bench. A black and red blaze on the head is permitted in competition in the USA. The patches show up very distinctly and should be vibrantly coloured.

The cat's nose leather and paw pads should be pink, black or both colours. The eyes should be brilliant copper or orange.

The Tortoiseshell and White (Calico) British Shorthair

Originally known as Chintz or Spanish Cats, the Tortie and White is now also known as the Calico. Ideally, this cat should display a well-distributed patching of black, red and cream on white. The white colour should not predominate. The nose leather and paw pads should be pink, black or both colours and the eyes a brilliant copper or orange.

There is also a Blue Tortie and White (Dilute Calico) in which blue replaces black and cream replaces red.

Above: *This is a Blue-Cream Shorthair which is also known as a Dilute Tortie. There should be no white hair in this breed. Another variety, the Dilute Calico, is a white cat with blue and cream patches.*

The Blue-Cream British Shorthair

The Blue-Cream British Shorthair is a form of Tortoiseshell in which cream replaces red and blue replaces black; making the Blue-Cream appear bi-coloured. It is a relative newcomer to the show bench, having been officially recognized in the UK in 1956.

The British standard demands that the coat be a soft intermingling of the two colours — this coat pattern is particularly attractive in the Persian Longhair, when the effect resembles that of shot-silk (see page 41). In addition, the palest shades of blue and cream are preferred, so it is easy to understand why the perfect Blue-Cream British Shorthair, according to UK standards, is comparatively rare. The US standard is similar, stipulating that the coat should be softly mingled. As with the British standard, the palest shades of blue and cream are preferred. Tabby markings or white hairs in the patches are a fault in the UK and the USA.

In the very young Blue-Cream British Shorthair kitten, it is difficult to determine the Blue-Cream from the solid Blue. The contrast becomes evident by the time the kitten is six months old. The cat's nose leather should be blue and the paw pads blue, pink or a combination of both. The Blue-Cream's eyes should be copper or orange.

Tortoiseshell and White British Shorthair

Tortoiseshell British Shorthair

Blue-Cream British Shorthair

Silver Spotted
Tabby British
Shorthair

Silver Classic
Tabby British
Shorthair kitten

*Illustrated here are examples of the
three tabby patterns: classic,
mackerel and spotted. The usual
colours associated with these
patterns in the British Shorthair are
brown, red and silver.*

Brown Mackerel
Tabby British
Shorthair

Red Classic
Tabby British
Shorthair

FACT FILE

●The name of 'tabby' is thought to
have originated from the similarity of
the cat's coat pattern to woven
watered silk or taffeta. The weaving of
this silk produces a striped effect on
the cloth which was known as
'tabbisilk' in England. The word
originates from a district in Baghdad
called Attabiya where this material
was manufactured.

●According to legend, the markings
on the forehead of the tabby form the
letter 'M' which stands for the prophet
Mahomet. The shoulder mark on the
classic tabby is said to be the imprint
left by Mahomet's hand when he
caressed his beloved cat.

Above: *This Silver Spotted Tabby clearly
shows its strongly contrasting coat pattern
which is similar to the mackerel pattern but
with stripes broken down into spots.*

Right: *This Brown Mackerel Tabby shows the
striking mackerel coat pattern. The markings
are much narrower than in the classic pattern
but both patterns have distinctive tabby rings.*

The Tabby British Shorthair

Tabby British Shorthairs have three coat patterns: classic, mackerel and spotted. All these patterns can occur in brown, silver, blue, red or cream colours. These three patterns, along with a combination of colours, can be found in other breeds besides the British Shorthair. Ideally, the contrast should be very strong between the base colour and the well-defined coat pattern.

The tabby pattern is the most common of all feline coat patterns. *Felis silvestris* and *Felis lybica*, ancestors of the domestic cat,

exhibited the mackerel (striped) coat pattern. The classic coat pattern was probably a mutation of this mackerel pattern. Among pedigree cats, the most common tabby coat is the classic coat pattern. Many non-pedigree cats have the tabby coat but with less defined markings than in the pedigree. The non-pedigree tabbies are usually varieties of either brown or red tabbies.

The tabby coat pattern is strengthened by matings between tabby and solid coloured cats. Tabby to tabby matings are often likely to deteriorate the pattern.

The Classic Tabby pattern is also called the blotched or marbled coat pattern. It should include 'necklaces', 'bracelets', and a ringed tail. Swirls should be present on the cheeks. An unbroken line runs from the outer corner of each eye. The head is marked with a pattern looking like the letter 'M' on the forehead. Vertical head markings should run from the 'M' to the shoulder markings which are in the shape of a butterfly. A 'bull's eye' or large blotch surrounded by two or more unbroken rings should appear on each flank. The two 'bull's eyes' should be identical.

The Red Classic Tabby is often dismissed as the 'marmalade' cat or 'ginger tom'. Nonetheless, this richly coloured cat is probably the most beautiful of all the colours. Contrary to some beliefs, not all Red Tabbies are male, although red to red matings do produce twice as many males. The coat colour should be a rich red with deep red markings. The chin and lips should be a darker red. The nose leather should be brick red, paw pads deep red and eyes copper.

The Mackerel Tabby has an unbroken line which runs down the spine. Narrow, unbroken lines should run vertically from the spine line. These lines should be clearly defined from the main coat colour. There should be fine 'pencillings' running outwards from the eye towards the back of the head to the shoulders. There is also an 'M' pattern on the forehead. This coat pattern should suggest a 'mackerel' cloud formation.

In the wild, the Brown Mackerel Tabby is quite common, but the pedigree equivalent is very rare. When the desired show standards are achieved, the Brown Tabby, with its round cobby head set squarely on to its massive body, is a splendid sight. The coat should be short and dense and the colour a rich copper brown with dense black tabby markings. The cat's chin and lips should be the same colour as the rings around the eyes. The hind legs, from paw to heel, should be black. The cat's nose leather should be brick red, the paw pads black and the eyes either orange or copper.

The Spotted Tabby dates back to Ancient Egyptian times and evidence of its existence has been found on Egyptian scrolls. The coat's spotted effect is caused by breaks in the classic tabby bars. The spots should be distinct and numerous and form round, oval or rosette shapes. The forehead should feature the distinctive tabby 'M' with an unbroken line running from the outer corner of each eye towards the back of the head. Fine 'pencillings' should appear on the cheeks. A stripe, broken by spots, runs down the spine. There should be a double row of spots on the chest and stomach with spots or broken stripes on the tail.

The Silver Spotted Tabby, with its gentle, loving nature and attractive 'smiling' face, is understandably one of the more popular of the British Shorthairs. The coat colour in the Silver should be a clear silvery grey with dense black markings. The chin and lips should be silver and the nose leather brick red or black. The paw pads should be black and the eyes green or hazel.

THE AMERICAN SHORTHAIR

The American Shorthair, formerly known as the Domestic Shorthair, is an independent, inquisitive and active creature. This breed of cat is robust and hardy.

This breed is more powerfully built than its British cousin and the coat is much firmer. It has a muscular, medium to large body with heavy shoulders and a well-developed chest. The cat's legs are strong and of medium length. The tail tapers from a thick base and has a blunt end. The large, well-proportioned head is slightly longer than it is wide. The American Shorthair has a square muzzle, full cheeks and medium-sized, slightly rounded ears. The eyes are large, round and slightly slanted at the outer edge.

There are approximately 25 varieties of the American Shorthair. Almost any colour and coat combination is possible: solid, bi-colour, van colour, tipped, shaded, smoke, tortie, torbie (patched tabby), and tabby.

The Silver Classic Tabby American Shorthair

The Silver Classic Tabby is the best known and most attractive of the American Shorthairs and is frequently held up as the most outstanding example of the breed.

The classic tabby coat pattern of the American Shorthair is the same as for the Classic Tabby British Shorthair (see page 29). The cat's coat colour, including the chin and lips, should be a pale, clear silver and the tabby markings should be dense black. The nose leather should be brick red and the paw pads should be black. The cat's eyes should be either green or hazel.

Shaded Silver American Shorthair

Silver Classic Tabby American Shorthair

Black Smoke American Wirehair

The Shaded Silver American Shorthair

Like its longhaired counterpart, the Shaded Persian (see page 39), the Shaded Silver American Shorthair has one-quarter of its hair length tipped with a dark colour. The undercoat of the Shaded Silver (shown above) should be white, and the black tipping should occur over the spine and shade to lighter tipping on either side of the body, finally disappearing altogether on the white underparts. The effect is of pewter rather than silver. There should be a black outline

Above: Both the American Shorthair and the American Wirehair have the same body shape and can be found in a wide variety of colours and coat patterns.

to the eye rims, lips and nose. The cat's nose leather should be brick red, the paw pads black and the eyes green or blue-green.

There is also a Shaded Cameo (Red) American Shorthair which has red tipping on a white undercoat. The Shaded Cameo is darker than the Shell Cameo variety.

THE EXOTIC SHORTHAIR

Mating the Persian Longhair with the American Shorthair was a deliberate move to create a Persian-type cat without the necessity for intense grooming. With its cobby body, short sturdy legs and round, massive head set on powerful shoulders, the Exotic Shorthair is closer to the British rather than the American Shorthair standard. The nose is short and snub and the eyes round and luminous. The small ears have rounded tips and are set wide apart on the head.

Initially bred from the Persian, the American Shorthair and the Burmese, the requirement now is for either one parent to be Persian and the other Exotic Shorthair, or both Exotic Shorthair.

Healthy, affectionate and similar in temperament to its Persian ancestors, the Exotic is a delightful companion with relatively few breeding problems. Exotic kittens are playful but not noisy. They are, on average, born four in a litter. Kittens are darker than their parents but coat texture and colour improve with age.

According to the CFA, the coat of the adult Exotic Shorthair should be plush, dense and soft to the touch, standing out from the body rather than lying flat or close. Medium in length, the coat should be slightly longer than that of other Shorthairs. All colours and coat patterns in the Persian and American Shorthair ranges are permitted.

THE AMERICAN WIREHAIR

In 1966, in up-state New York, two farm cats produced a litter of kittens, one of which had a strange 'wiry' coat. This red and white male kitten and one of its normal litter-mates were bought by a breeder who eventually mated both cats to each other. The ensuing litter, born in 1967, contained four kittens. Two of these were red and white, just like their father. It was decided to call this new variety of cat the American Wirehair.

Given official championship status by the CFA in 1977, the Wirehair is one of the few breeds of cat which is truly native to the United States. Standards are the same as for the American Shorthair except that the round head should have prominent cheekbones, a slight whisker break and a nose which is gently concave in profile.

All hairs on the Wirehair are crimped, springy to the touch and hooked at the ends — even in the ears. The whiskers are also crimped and wavy and spring at untidy angles from the muzzle. The hair on longer-coated American Wirehairs is of the same texture but forms long ringlets of fur. The Wirehair is intelligent, actively curious and agile. Virtually any colour or coat pattern is accepted for competition.

Above: *The American Wirehair, seen here, displays the 'wiry' coat which first appeared as a natural mutation. The hair on the chin, chest and stomach is slightly less coarse than on the rest of its body.*

The Shaded Cameo Exotic has shorter hair than the Shaded Cameo Persian. It was bred from Persian and Shorthair parents and has a medium-length coat.

Shaded Cameo Exotic Shorthair

LONGHAIRED CATS

In the 16th Century, the first longhaired cats reached Europe. The Angora from Turkey is considered to be one of the most ancient breeds of cat and was probably the first to arrive in the West. Allegedly, the Angora was brought to France from Turkey by a French scientist named Nicholas Fabri de Peirese. Meanwhile, a similar breed developed around the Lake Van area of Turkey and became known as the Turkish Van.

From neighbouring Persia (Iran) came another longhaired breed, more sturdy in appearance than the Turkish breeds. It became known as the Persian. Most often in the white variety, these cats were first seen in Italy, then in France, probably brought to these countries by travellers and merchants. By the end of the 16th Century, the Angora had reached Britain from France and the Persian shortly followed. They were both known for a time as French cats in Britain, due to their previous residence in France.

In the early 18th Century, the French naturalist De Buffon noted that there were cats with long fur in Asia Minor. However, it was not until the 19th Century that any real interest in the longhairs was shown and the Turkish Angora — as it was then known — the Persian and another longhaired cat, the Russian Longhair, were recorded.

The Persian was introduced to America toward the end of the 19th Century and subsequently became the most desired variety of longhaired cat both there and in Europe. The Turkish breeds fell from favour until the mid 1950s when devotees of the breeds began to promote them further.

In Britain, all Persian-type longhaired cats are grouped and judged under the name of Longhair and each colour is classified as a breed. The Birman, Angora, Turkish Van and Colourpoints are also classified as different breeds under the Longhair heading.

In North America, Persians are one breed with their colours judged as variations of that breed. Other cats such as Angoras, Turkish Vans, Birmans, Main Coon Cats and Norwegian Forest Cats are judged as separate breeds from Persians.

Right: *These beautiful Norwegian Forest Cats are a Red Bi-colour and a Smoke. Each shows the ideal triangular head shape, long straight nose and full cheeks. Generous ear tufts can be seen in the upright, pointed ears.*

THE NORWEGIAN FOREST CAT

The Norwegian Forest Cat or Norsk Skaukatt is a large, natural breed of cat from Norway which has for many years played an important role in the folklore of that country.

Despite its wild-sounding name, this cat has, at least since its discovery, lived on the borders of human habitation. Being an intelligent and sociable type of cat, it quickly adapted to domestication, recently progressing to become an established pedigree breed. Recognized by the FIFe (Fédération Internationale Féline d'Europe), the Forest Cat is registered but only at preliminary status in the UK. However, TICA in America has given this breed full status.

Like many breeds which have naturally evolved, the Norwegian Forest Cat is hardy and well-suited to its environment. It is, by nature, a good hunter and climber.

This cat is long (medium-long by US standards) in body and leg which gives the impression of power and strength. The hind legs are higher than the front legs. Its shaggy coat is ideal for the harsh Norwegian climate. A protective ruff of fur appears in autumn and disappears the following summer. The cat has a thick undercoat and its guard hairs (topcoat) are of a smooth texture.

Any colour or coat pattern is now accepted but the usual coat pattern is the tabby. The chest and ear tufts are creamy white and white often appears on the paws. The nose leather, paw pads and eye colour should correspond to the coat colour.

FACT FILE

● The robust and hardy Norwegian Forest Cat loves to climb high trees and comes down head first.

● Norwegian Forest Cats have almost 'waterproof' coats which dry quickly and protect them from rain.

● A popular story is that the Maine Coon Cat originated from a mating between a farm cat and a racoon — hence the name!

● One of the largest breeds of domestic cat, the Maine Coon Cat can weigh as much as 7 kg (15lb).

Brown Tabby and White Norwegian Forest Cat

Blue and White Bi-colour Maine Coon Cat

Above: *Both the Maine Coon Cat and the Norwegian Forest Cat enjoy the outdoors, are active, hardy and good mousers.*

THE MAINE COON CAT

The Maine Coon Cat has been recognized as a unique breed in its native state of Maine, USA, since the 19th Century. Most authorities believe it originated from Angora and American Shorthair parents.

The Maine Coon Cat was first exhibited in Maine in 1861. It gained considerable interest at the New York cat show in 1895. Its popularity dwindled due to the influx of Persians until the Maine Coon Cat Club was formed in 1953. Also popular in the UK, the Maine Coon is registered with the GCCF.

The Maine Coon Cat has a long head with high cheekbones and large, tufted ears. It is long-bodied and muscular with a broad chest and level back. The fur is shorter at the shoulders, becoming longer as it reaches the tail. All colours and coat patterns are permitted for competition as are any combinations of coat and eye colour.

FACT FILE

• The uniquely coloured Turkish Van has been kept as a domestic pet for centuries in its homeland of Turkey where it enjoys swimming in the mountain lakes and streams.

• The Angora cat derived its name from the Turkish city of Angora (Ankara). The word 'angora' is used to describe the soft long fur or wool which can be found on goats and rabbits as well as cats.

THE ANGORA

The Angora was the first longhaired cat to be seen in Europe. It originated in the city of Angora (now called Ankara) in Turkey. This cat has a small head, tallish ears, a lithe body and a longish, tapering tail. The longhaired cat from Persia, which arrived in Europe after the Angora, had longer hair, a sturdier body and a rounder head. These Persian Longhairs eventually gained much more popularity than the Angora. However, the fur of the Angora, although long, has no woolly undercoat like the Persian. This makes the Angora easier to groom. The Angora arrived in Britain at the end of the 16th Century.

In their homeland of Turkey, the Angoras are known by various names — according to their colour. For instance, the red tabby variety is known as the *sarman*; the silver tabby is the *teku* and the odd-eyed white bears the romantic name of *Ankara kedi*. In Turkey, the Angora is seen in many colours and coat patterns but the White is said to be the only true Angora. The Ankara Zoo once established a breeding colony of White Angoras in an effort to preserve them. In 1963, these Angoras were taken from the zoo to America where they were called Turkish Angoras. Although Angoras have mainly been developed as a white cat outside Turkey, many other colours are now produced and accepted for competition.

Despite being a longhaired cat, the accepted colour range for the Angora in Britain is listed in the Shorthair Register along with the Exotics and Foreign and Oriental Shorthairs of Siamese type. The GCCF requires the nose tip, pads and inside of ears of the White to be a delicate shell pink.

Amber-eyed White Angora

The Angora and Turkish Van are ancient breeds of cat from Turkey. The Angora is most popular in white, although other colours exist — either naturally or man-made.

Turkish Van

Turkish Van kitten

This beautiful cat with medium to long silky hair has a full, feathery tail which is often wavy. The CFA show standard for the Turkish Angora requires the cat to have a graceful and flowing movement.

Today's Angora is a small to medium-sized cat with a long, graceful body. The legs are long with small round paws. The long tail is often held upright and curled over the body. The wedge-shaped head has tall, pointed ears and large, almond-shaped eyes. The nose is medium long and straight. The nose leather and paw pads correspond to the coat colour, and the eyes should be amber or green except in the White when they should be blue or odd-eyed.

These cats have a gentle disposition, and are loyal and affectionate. They are dainty, graceful and, although quiet, quite alert and lively. They easily adapt to their surroundings so they would suit either country or town living.

THE TURKISH VAN

The Turkish Van was originally domesticated in its native land of Turkey. It is a truly distinctive animal — both in its appearance and in its love of swimming. In America, this breed is known as the Turkish Van or Turkish cat but in Britain its official name is the Turkish cat. Throughout the United States and Europe, it is also commonly referred to as 'the swimming cat'.

In 1955, a breeding pair of Turkish Vans were presented to two British cat-lovers holidaying in Turkey. The pair were brought back to Britain where they attracted much attention. As no official records had been kept in Turkey with regards to breeding, it was necessary to produce three generations of pure breeding before the cats were finally officially recognized in Britain in 1969. Breeders then became interested and the Van reached the USA in the late 1970s. However, the breed is still comparatively rare.

The Turkish Van breeds true, producing kittens that always resemble the parents. Even from birth, the Turkish Van kitten displays auburn (red in the USA) markings to the head and tail. The Van's main coat colour is chalky white. The long, fine coat (in the USA it is described as semi-long) becomes longer in winter and is not fully

Above: These Angoras (on the left Cinnamon and on the right Blue Tabby) are good examples of their breed. They show the wedge-shaped head with wide-based, long, pointed ears and almond-shaped eyes.

Below: The Turkish Van is one of the very few cats that like to swim. Since it originated from the mountainous areas of the great Lake Van in Turkey, this is hardly surprising. Here is one really enjoying the water!

developed until a kitten reaches the adult stage. In the adult, the main coat colour should have no hint of yellow. The auburn (red) face markings appear between the ears and the eyes, and extend across the forehead. The nose, cheeks and chin are white. The tail (called the brush in the USA) is auburn (red) in colour with faint ring markings — these are more prominent in the kitten.

The Turkish Van is similar in build to the Angora. It has a long body but is slightly sturdier. It has medium-length legs and neat, round feet with well-tufted toes. The tail is full and medium in length. The head is short and wedge-shaped with large, upright ears set fairly close together and tufted. The eyes should be round, light amber in colour and have pink-skinned rims. The nose, paw pads and the inside of the ear should be pink.

The soft, silky coat (in the USA the coat is described as silky to hard), with no woolly undercoat, should present few problems to the caring owner. Grooming should be carried out daily, but the coat is easily maintained. If a pre-show bath is required, this is not a problem! The Turkish Van takes great pleasure in being bathed, providing that the water is kept to its own temperature which is about 38°C (101°F). The Van should be towel dried briskly and thoroughly after bathing or swimming sessions.

TICA, the ACFA (American Cat Fancy Association), the CFA and the GCCF have all accepted the Turkish Van for competition. The GCCF recognizes a Cream Turkish in addition to the original Turkish colour combination of auburn and white. In the USA, there are also Black and White, Cream and White, and Calico varieties.

THE PERSIAN LONGHAIR

In the UK, this breed of cat is officially called a Longhair and each colour is regarded as a different breed. However, it is simply called the Persian in the USA, and all the different colours are variations of the breed. Most people, however, commonly refer to it as a Persian.

The Persian Longhair is a companionable and docile pet. It is not as adventurous as some other breeds which makes it well suited for flat or apartment living. It does require daily grooming.

Within the Persian group, there are now some 53 varieties, reflecting a wide range of colours and coat patterns. The body build remains much the same for all varieties. The build is cobby, massive, and set on short legs. The coat is long and flowing and the tail short and full. The broad, round head has small, well-tufted ears, a short nose and full cheeks. The eyes are full, large and round.

The White Persian Longhair

When the first cat shows were held in the 19th Century, the White Persian began to attract a lot of attention. This magnificent longhair became everyone's idea of a true pedigree cat. They were a fashionable status symbol and lady members of the British aristocracy set up breeding establishments. Meanwhile, White Persians were greatly sought after in America and were entered in cat shows there.

Today, the GCCF standard requires the White Persian's coat colour to be a pure, glistening white. The cat's nose leather and paw pads should be pink and the eye colour deep blue or copper. In the case of the odd-eyed White, the eyes should each show equal depth of colour.

The Black Persian Longhair

Although white was considered to be the original Persian Longhair colour, Black Persians were also known in Europe at the end of the 16th Century. They were eventually seen on the British show bench in 1871.

Today, the Black Persian should have a dense, coal-black coat, sound in colour from the roots to the tips of the fur. The coat must be free from any 'rustiness' or discolouration. A good specimen is difficult to attain — its coat can be bleached by the sun or look at its worst during moulting.

This cat's nose leather should be black and the paw pads black or brown. The eyes should be a brilliant copper.

All colour varieties of the Persian (called the Longhair in Britain) have the same body shape. These cats are docile and quiet but need daily grooming to prevent matting and to keep their coats fluffy.

Black Persian

White Persian

FACT FILE

● Despite its cobby build and short legs, the Persian is relatively agile.

● Persians must be groomed daily to avoid painful matting and furballs which may form in the stomach if the cat swallows too much fur.

● The fact that Queen Victoria was very fond of her three Blue Persians undoubtedly did much to popularize and promote the breed.

● The Persian is a quiet, docile pet but it dislikes being teased.

Blue Persian

Black and White
Bi-colour Persian

Cream
Persian
kitten

Red Persian

Above; *This beautiful Red and White Bi-colour Perisan shows distinct and symmetrical patches, in particular, the display of colour around the face.*

The Blue Persian Longhair

The Blue first appeared when early Whites were bred with Black Persians. Blue Persians were first shown in Britain under their own separate classes in 1889.

According to the GCCF, coat colour is, preferably, a light shade of blue with an even tone from the nose to the tip of the tail. The colour must be solid to the roots. If the desired lighter shade is patchy, then a sound darker shade is preferable. The Blue Persian should have blue nose leather and paw pads and brilliant copper eyes.

The Red Persian Longhair

The glorious coat of the solid Red Persian is probably the most difficult to achieve to perfection. In both the UK and the USA, the coat is required to be a deep rich red with no markings but, because the red colour is usually associated with the tabby pattern, markings are often apparent. Another factor which makes the Red difficult to produce is that red colouring is passed down to the males, making the red female uncommon. The nose leather and paw pads should be brick red and the eye colour deep copper.

The Cream Persian Longhair

Creams were first seen in Britain in the 1890s but were regarded as Reds that were too pale to be judged — so they were usually just kept as pets and not allowed in competitions. A serious breeding programme for Creams was not established until the 1920s in Britain.

As with the Cream Shorthair, the colour must not be too reddish. A paler cream is preferable in America but a medium cream is permissible in Britain. The coat should be solid in colour with no pale undercoat.

The Bi-colour Persian Longhair

The Bi-colour used to be regarded as a common alley cat of dubious parentage. Only comparatively recently has it appeared on the show bench as a recognized variety.

The bi-colour coat was formerly based on the Dutch coat pattern in which white areas were confined to the underparts. This Dutch coat standard was found to be difficult to achieve, so appropriate revisions were made. The GCCF standard for the bi-colour pattern requires the patches of colour to be evenly distributed throughout the coat with no tabby markings or white hairs among the colour patches. No more than two thirds of the coat should be coloured and no more than half should be white. The face should be patched with colour and white.

Many colour varieties are accepted in Britain; there is an even wider range in the USA.

FACT FILE

● The South American rodent called the Chinchilla has a coat that is dark at the roots and white at the tips — this is the opposite of the Chinchilla cat's coat.

● The Chinchilla Persian is famed for its appearances in magazines and films. It also appears on television advertisements where it promotes items ranging from carpets to cat food.

● Smoke Persian kittens which develop a pale undercoat most quickly will usually become the best coloured adult Smokes.

The Chinchilla and Shell Cameo Persian Longhair

There are three main types of tipped coat pattern: Shell and Chinchilla, Shaded, and Smoke. Of these, the Shell and Chinchilla group has the lightest tipping. All three types have a white, or sometimes cream, undercoat with the guard hairs (top coat) tipped to varying lengths with another, darker colour. In the Chinchilla and the Shell Cameo only one-eighth of the hair length is tipped. This produces a shimmering effect.

The Chinchilla Persian has been known since the 1890s and was thought to be derived from Silver Tabbies which had almost non-existent markings. These cats were much acclaimed and gained even further popularity in the 1930s when Queen Victoria's granddaughter, the Princess Victoria, became interested in them.

The Chinchilla has a long and dense coat of a fine, silky texture. The undercoat is pure white and the topcoat is tipped with black on the flanks, head, ears and tail which gives the coat a sparkling silver effect. The nose leather should be brick red. The paw pads and the visible skin on the eyelids should be black. The large, expressive eyes are emerald or blue-green in colour. The Chinchilla should be slightly more fine-boned than the Persian Longhair by British standards but, in the USA, it has the same body standard as the Persian. Of a similar colour combination, the Masked Silver Chinchilla has light tipping on the back, flanks and tail and heavier tipping on the face and paws.

The Golden Chinchilla or Golden Persian is a new variety of Chinchilla. According to the US standard, this lovely cat has a cream undercoat with seal brown tipping. The British standard describes the undercoat as apricot deepening to gold. The nose leather should be deep rose for the US standard but should be brick red for the UK standard. The paw pads should be dark brown and the eyes emerald or blue-green.

The Shell Cameo was produced by mating Silver Tabbies with Red Persians. This breed is also known as the Red Chinchilla. The Shell Cameo's coat has a sparkling pink 'tinsel' appearance. This breed has a white undercoat with a very light tipping of red to give a rose-pink tone. The GCCF describes the coat as being sparkling silver dusted with rose pink. The nose leather and paw pads should be rose. The eyes should be brilliant copper outlined in rose.

The Cameo Tabby has an undercoat of cream or off-white with the guard hairs lightly tipped with red in either the classic or mackerel tabby pattern. Like the Shell Cameo, the Cameo Tabby should have rose nose leather and paw pads. The eyes should be a brilliant copper.

Other varieties of the Shell Cameo are the Tortoiseshell and the Blue-Cream.

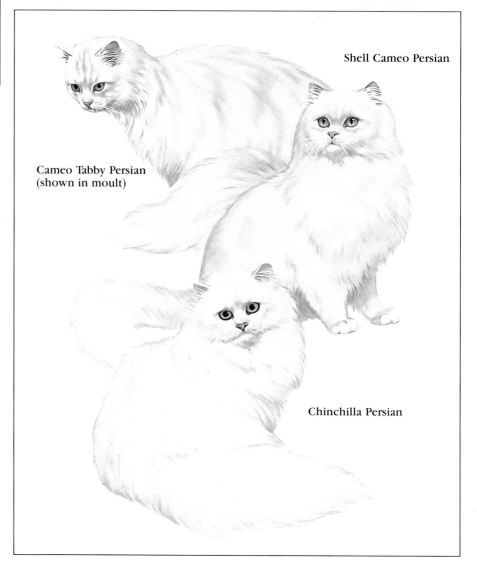

Shell Cameo Persian

Cameo Tabby Persian
(shown in moult)

Chinchilla Persian

Shaded Cameo Persian

Shaded Silver Persian

Blue Smoke Persian

The Shaded Persian Longhair

The Shaded Persian is very similar to the Chinchilla and Shell but the tipping covers one-quarter of the hair length. This extra depth of colour gives the cat the appearance of wearing a mantle or cloak.

The Shaded Cameo has a red tipping on the back, flanks, face, legs and tail, and the undercoat is white. The nose leather and paw pads should be rose and the eyes should be copper rimmed in rose.

A slightly darker version of the American Shaded Silver is known as the Pewter in Britain. Both have pure white undercoats but the American version has a lesser degree of black tipping. Both should have brick red noses outlined in black and paw pads which are black or dark brown. The Shaded Silver has black-rimmed green or green-blue eyes and the Pewter has black-rimmed orange or copper eyes.

There are now other varieties such as the Shaded Golden and the Shaded Tortie.

The Smoke Persian Longhair

The Smoke Persians have the most heavily tipped coats. They give the appearance of a self coloured cat but, when they move, the pale undercoat shows through. Both the Black and its dilute form, the Blue Smoke, have ash-white undercoats with tipping that is at least one-half the length of each hair.

In the Blue Smoke, the blue hairs shade gradually to white. The nose leather and the paw pads should be blue and the eyes brilliant orange or copper.

In the Black Smoke, the tipping shades to silver on the lower flanks. The face and the feet should be solidly black in the UK, but in the USA there should be white at the roots. The nose leather and paw pads should be black and the eyes orange or copper. Other varieties of Smoke include the Cameo (Red) Smoke and the Tortoiseshell Smoke.

Above: Shaded and Smoke coats are more heavily tipped than the Chinchilla or Cameo. However, Shaded kittens can appear in the same litters as Chinchillas and Cameos.

Left: The delicate colouring of these cats belies the fact that they are healthy and strong. Kittens of the Shell Cameo are born white and their tips later darken to red.

Right: Americans call the Chinchilla a Silver Persian which aptly describes this truly fairy-tale cat with its sparkling silver coat and emerald green eyes.

The Tabby Persian Longhair

Tabby is a 'naturally' occuring coat pattern that has been seen for centuries in the wild cat and the early domestic cat. Some early tabby cats had shaggy, medium-length fur which was environmentally induced — for instance, in cold, mountainous regions the cat would naturally grow longer hair in order to keep warm. However, it was not until the 19th Century that shorthaired tabbies were selectively bred with longhaired cats to produce the distinctive Tabby Persian Longhair.

Tabby Longhairs have long been a favourite with cat-lovers and, at the cat shows of over a hundred years ago, special classes were held for them in Britain. In those days, the Silver Tabby was probably the most popular breed. The Browns, or the 'Brownies' as they were affectionately named, followed a close second. Enthusiasts applauded the Brown's 'rich sable ground colouring and dense black markings'. The Blue Tabby, also described at the early shows, is not now recognized in the UK but the American cat fancy still includes the Blue Tabby in their show standards.

There are two basic types of tabby coat pattern that occur in the Longhair: the classic and the mackerel (for pattern description see Tabby Shorthairs, page 28-29). In Britain, the GCCF recognizes only the classic (blotched) coat pattern, and this is simply classified as 'Tabby'. The American cat fancy recognizes both the classic and the mackerel coat pattern. In addition, some American associations recognize a Patched Tabby or a Torbie (Tortoiseshell and Tabby).

Tabby Persian kittens are usually born with very strong tabby markings. However, not all kittens are destined for the show bench — many, with indistinct markings or incorrect ground colour, make delightful pets.

Brown Classic Tabby Persian

Silver Classic Tabby Persian

Red Mackerel Tabby Persian

Left: *Tabby Persian Longhairs have three basic coat colours — Brown, Silver and Red. Other shades are derived from these.*

Officially recognized colour varieties are: the Brown Tabby or 'Brownie', which has a ground colour of rich, tawny sable with jet black markings; the Red Tabby, which is rich red with darker red; the Silver Tabby, which is silver with jet black; the Blue Tabby, which is pale bluish-ivory with slate blue; the Cream Tabby, which is pale cream with rich cream; and the Cameo Tabby, which is off-white with red.

The Tabby Persian has the same body build as all Persian Longhairs. The coat is flowing and long. The silky fur produces a softer and more 'fluid' tabby pattern than on the Shorthairs. The tail is short and full. The broad, round head has small, well-tufted ears, a short, broad nose and full cheeks. The deep ruff or 'frill', the underparts and the cheeks and ear tufts are lighter in colour than the rest of the body.

The Tortoiseshell Persian and its dilute form, the Blue-Cream, are both female-only breeds.

Tortoiseshell Persian

Blue-Cream Persian

The Blue-Cream Persian Longhair

The Blue-Cream is a dilute of the Tortoiseshell and is often referred to as a Dilute Tortie or Blue Tortie. Blue replaces the black colour and cream replaces the red. Essentially, its colours are blue, cream and cream, which makes the patches look bi-coloured rather than tri-coloured.

The body standard is the same as for all Persian Longhairs. The nose leather and paw pads should be pink or blue or both and the eyes deep copper or orange.

The Tortoiseshell and White (Calico) Persian Longhair

The Tortie and White is commonly known as the Calico Persian. The colour is the same as for the Tortoiseshell, except with the addition of white. This makes the cat red, black, cream and white. The patches should be evenly distributed and the colours bright. In the USA, cat associations usually prefer the white patches to be limited to the underparts of the cat. This is known as the Dutch coat pattern.

There is also a dilute of the Tortie and White in which blue replaces black and cream replaces white so the colours are: blue, cream and white. This breed is known as the Blue Tortoiseshell and White, the Dilute Tortie and White or the Dilute Calico. A Van Calico is permitted for competition in the USA. The coloured patches appear on the head and tail as in the Turkish Van cat.

Right: *This Silver Tabby, seen here among sun-dappled grasses and vegetation, demonstrates how well the tabby coat pattern can act as camouflage in nature.*

The Tortoiseshell Persian Longhair

The first Tortoiseshell Longhair was recorded around the turn of the century. It was thought to have been brought about by matings between Black Persians and short-haired tortoiseshell barnyard cats. They first appeared in cat shows in the United States and Britain at this time but were usually of unknown parentage. They became very popular in both Europe and the USA but they are difficult to breed.

They are, like the Tortie Shorthair (see page 27), tri-coloured: red, black and cream, with the patches clearly defined. The body build is the same as for the Persian Longhair. Often tabby markings appear with the Tortie. In the United States, these are called Patched Tabbies or Torbies and they are officially accepted patterns.

Right: The Colourpoint (Himalayan) is a longhaired cat with coloured points like the pure Siamese. Until recently, the self coloured Colourpoint Persian was called the Kashmir in the United States of America.

Lilac Self Coloured Colourpoint

Tortie-point Colourpoint

Seal-point Colourpoint

THE COLOURPOINT (HIMALAYAN) LONGHAIR

Known as the Colourpoint in Britain and the Himalayan in the USA, this breed was the result of deliberate attempts by breeders to bring Siamese 'points' to the Persian cat. This was done by mating Persians with Siamese. In North America, the Himalayan is classified as a colour variation of the Persian by the CFA but as a Himalayan Persian, a separate breed, by TICA. In the UK, the Colourpoint is grouped with other longhaired cats under the general heading of Longhairs.

The Colourpoint resembles the Siamese only in colour. It has a body of true Persian standard (see page 36). The coat should be long and thick with a fine glossy texture. Frequent grooming of the coat is necessary. The nose should be short and snub with no hint of the long, straight Siamese nose.

There are approximately 20 varieties of the Colourpoint. The breed's colours and coat patterns are the same as for the Siamese (see pages 44-46). The nose leather and paw pads correspond to the coat colour and the eyes should be a deep brilliant blue. The cat was recognized by the GCCF in 1955; its American counterpart gained the same status by the CFA in 1957.

THE SELF COLOURED COLOURPOINT (HIMALAYAN) LONGHAIR

During the Colourpoint (Himalayan) breeding programme, it was inevitable that some self or solid coloured cats should appear. Until recently, these were called Kashmirs in the USA, and judged as self coloured Himalayans. The CFA in America now groups them as self coloured Persians, as does the GCCF in Britain. TICA, however, groups them as a separate breed, the Himalayan Persian, which encompasses both the 'pointed' and the solid Himalayan.

The first self coloured Colourpoints were Chocolate. Today, the standard requires the coat to be an even colour of rich, warm chocolate brown, sound from roots to the tips of the fur. This is difficult to produce because chocolate coats are often found to fade or bleach. There is also a dilute form of chocolate which is lilac.

Body standards are the same as for the Colourpoint (Himalayan) Longhair. The nose leather and paw pads should be brown in the Chocolate and pink in the Lilac. The eyes in both varieties should be copper.

THE BIRMAN

The Birman is also known as the Sacred Cat of Burma but should in no way be confused with the shorthaired Burmese cat.

According to legend, many years before Buddha, the temples of the Khmer people of Burma were guarded by white longhaired cats with golden eyes. One of these cats, named Sinh, was the personal favourite of Mun-Ha, High Priest in the Lao-Tsun temple of the goddess Tsun-Kyan-Kse. One day, as Mun-Ha knelt before the golden figure of the blue-eyed goddess, he was killed by invaders. The cat Sinh leapt upon his master's body and faced the eyes of the goddess. On doing so, the soul of Mun-Ha passed into the cat. The cat's white fur transformed to gold and its eyes to a brilliant blue — reflecting the colours of the goddess. Its legs turned golden but the feet, as they rested on the body of the priest, remained white.

This Seal-point Birman shows the 'gloved' forepaws and 'gauntleted' back paws which are unique to the breed.

Seal-point Birman

The Birman is a majestic-looking longhaired (semi-longhaired by US standards) cat with a pale body and darker coloured points — in this case the points being the mask, ears, tail and legs. Differing from other 'pointed' cats (the Siamese, for example), the Birman's paws are white. The four main point colours are seal, blue, chocolate and lilac. From these, breeders have derived a wide range of colours, all of which can be either solid or in the tabby and tortie coat patterns. The main body colour of the Seal-point is beige or cream. The main colour of the Blue-point is bluish-white; in the Chocolate-point it is ivory and in the Lilac-point it is white. The nose leathers are, respectively: brown, grey, cinnamon-pink and lavender-pink. The paw pads should be pink and the eye colour blue — the deeper and more violet the blue, the better. Throughout all colour and coat patterns, the characteristic white Birman paws prevail.

Though similar in build to the Persian, the Birman is longer in the body with proportionately longer legs and tail. The head is fairly round and broad with full cheeks and medium-sized, round-tipped ears. The Birman's eyes are round and the nose is longer and straighter than the Persian's.

The Birman was given recognition in France in 1925, in the UK in 1966 and in the USA in 1967.

Left: *The seal-pointed mask and ears form a perfect setting for the brilliant blue eyes of this lovely Birman.*

FOREIGN AND ORIENTAL BREEDS

Many breeds of cat are described as being 'oriental' in type, a description which refers to their general shape rather than their origins, although some breeds do originate from the Far East. Oriental type cats tend to have short sleek coats, slim elegant bodies with long legs and a long tapering tail, wedge-shaped heads, large pointed ears and almond-shaped eyes. The best known of the oriental cats is the Siamese, from which many other breeds, such as the Balinese and Tonkinese, are derived. Another close relative of the Siamese is known as the Oriental Shorthair in the USA and the Foreign Shorthair in Britain.

Other breeds, such as the Abyssinian, Burmese and Russian Blue, are described as being of 'modified' oriental type, the oriental characteristics being less distinguished than in the Siamese and Foreign Shorthairs.

In Britain, all these various breeds of cat are grouped together and judged under the general heading of 'Foreigns', whereas in the USA the breeds remain divided into their own special classes. Other US breeds in this section include the Bombay, Snowshoe, Havana Brown, Egyptian Mau, Singapura and Somali, none of which are fully recognized in Britain.

THE SIAMESE

The origins of the Siamese are interwoven with the mysteries of south-eastern Asia. In Ayudha, ancient capital city of Siam (Thailand), there dwelt a variety of cat that was much-valued by the people of that city. This is known from an ancient manuscript, the *Cat-Book Poems,* which describes and depicts these early 'Siamese'. Legend has it that these cats were the 'Royal Cats of Siam', and that they were well-respected and lived in the temples and royal palaces. One amusing story tells how they guarded religious treasures in the city's temples so closely and for so long that their eyes began to squint.

Throughout the years, and even today, some Siamese still show a squint which, while being part of the Siamese make-up, is considered to be a fault on the show bench.

It is recorded that Siamese cats were seen at one of the first British cat shows in 1871. Regarded with curiosity and some reluctance at first, the Siamese rapidly gained popularity, although some people believed that the cats were too delicate for Britain's colder climate. The breed arrived in North America in 1890, and in 1892 the first British standard was established. Since then, revisions of this standard have resulted in the more svelte, elegant Siamese cat of today.

The Siamese is a very popular pet, being elegant, intelligent, affectionate and companionable. However, it does demand a lot of attention and can be quite noisy.

The body of the Siamese is medium in size, long and svelte with long, slender legs. The hind legs are slightly longer than the front legs and the paws are small and oval. The tail,

Above: *This Blue-point Siamese has the required British standard — a 'glacial' (ice-like) white coat and clearly defined points of slate blue. Its eyes are a deep vivid blue.*

Right: *In America, the coat of the Lilac-point Siamese is a 'glacial' white but the UK standards require a warmer, 'magnolia' shade. The points are pinkish-grey and the eyes, like the Blue-point, are deep vivid blue.*

Seal-point Siamese

Lilac-point Siamese kitten

Blue-point Siamese kitten

Chocolate-point Siamese

FACT FILE

●The Foreign and Oriental breeds, particularly the Siamese, take readily to harness and lead.

●Siamese cats love games and performing tricks and they love to talk, almost endlessly.

●The Siamese is loyal and often possessive towards its owner.

●Supposedly a gift from the King of Siam, the first Siamese cats were brought to England in 1884 by the British Consul General of Bangkok.

Left: *The Seal-point, the Blue-point, the Chocolate-point and the Lilac-point seen here display the four basic point colours of the Siamese breed.*

should not have a greenish tinge. The nose and paw pads should be black or seal brown.

Over the last fifty years, other point colours have emerged. There are three other main point colours: Blue-point, Chocolate-point, and Lilac-point. Of the four basic Siamese point colours, the original Seal-point is still the most popular.

In the Blue-point, the body is a glacial bluish-white, shading to darker blue on the back and white on the stomach and chest. The points are a dark slate blue. The eyes should be clear, bright and a vivid blue and the nose leather and paw pads slate blue. The Chocolate-point's coat is an all-over ivory shade with points of a milk chocolate colour. The eyes should be a clear, vivid blue and the leathers a pinky chocolate.

The Lilac-point's body colour is magnolia in the UK and glacial white in the USA, with pinkish-grey points. The eyes should be a deep vivid blue and the leathers pinkish-grey. Kittens in all colours are born white with points begining to show at four to six weeks, becoming clearly defined when the kitten is nine months old.

In Britain, many other point colours are accepted in the Siamese breed. The American breed standard, however, varies. The CFA only recognizes the four main point colours, and other varieties are judged under Colourpoint Shorthairs.

which is sometimes called a 'whip', is long and tapering and in proportion to the rest of the body. Siamese cats have the characteristic coat pattern of a pale body with darker contrasting 'points'. The 'points', where the darker colour occurs, are the face mask, ears, legs and tail. These cats have often been used in selective breeding programmes to create 'points' in other breeds, for example, the Colourpoint Longhair or Himalayan (see page 42) is derived from selective breeding of Siamese and Persian Longhairs.

The original Siamese cat was a Seal-point, although the points were a much darker shade than we know today. Seal is a brown colour which is a dilution of black. The Seal-point Siamese is a particularly distinctive looking cat with a cream body shading to a warm fawn on the back and a lighter colour on the stomach and chest. The points are clearly defined and dark seal brown in colour. The eyes, as with other Siamese varieties, are a deep vivid blue, oriental in shape and slanting towards the nose. There should be no tendency to squint and the eyes

Above: This Chocolate Tabby-point Siamese (Lynx-point Colourpoint) is a hybrid breed derived from Chocolate-point Siamese and Tabby Shorthair parents.

Right: These cats all derived their colour variations from the four main Siamese varieties and other Shorthair parents.

Other Siamese (Colourpoint Shorthairs)

Many people believe that the only true Siamese is the traditional Seal-point with its derivitives Lilac-, Chocolate- and Blue-points. They believe that cats with other colours and coat patterns should be called by another name. Indeed, the CFA in America does call all Siamese cats with point colours other than seal, lilac, chocolate and blue, Colourpoint Shorthairs. However, in Britain and in most other North American cat associations, these cats are still called Siamese. Whatever the name, many new colours and coat patterns have been developed within the Siamese range over the last fifty years.

During the late 1940s, breeding programmes in the United States produced a Red-point Siamese. Shortly afterwards came a Tortoiseshell-point — in all the classic shades of seal, blue, chocolate and lilac. The Cream-point followed.

In 1960, a British Seal-point Siamese mated with a roving tabby tom and produced a single tabby kitten among her litter of Seal-points. The tabby was female and was mated

back to a Seal-point male. Out of the resulting litter, four of the kittens had tabby points! Amid much interest, this striking new breed was recognized by the GCCF in 1966 and the CFA shortly afterwards. Many felt that the name Lynx-point suited this stripe-pointed cat. Although the British chose to call it the Tabby-point Siamese, the name Lynx-point was selected in America.

In addition to the four basic point colours, the Siamese (Colourpoint Shorthair) colours and coat patterns are as follows: Red-point; Cream-point; Seal Tortie-point; Chocolate Tortie-point; Blue-Cream-point; Lilac-Cream-point; Seal Tabby-point; Chocolate Tabby-point; Blue Tabby-point; Lilac Tabby-point; Red Tabby-point; Cream Tabby-point and Torbie-point (tortoiseshell and tabby). Standards for each of these remain the same as in the Siamese range.

THE SNOWSHOE

The Snowshoe is a 'pointed' cat which has recently been developed by North American breeders. This hybrid breed is the result of

Blue-point Snowshoe

Chocolate Tabby-point Colourpoint Shorthair

Red-point Colourpoint Shorthair

Chocolate Tortie-point Colourpoint Shorthair kitten

The Blue-point Balinese has the same colour standard as the Blue-point Siamese. The Balinese is derived from longhaired cats born to normal shorthaired Siamese parents.

Blue-point Balinese

THE BALINESE

In the United States in the 1950s, longhaired kittens appeared in some pure-bred Siamese litters. Although similar to their litter-mates in every respect except for their long hair, breeders were convinced that these were abnormal Siamese, so many were neutered, sold as pets or destroyed. They were, in fact, naturally occuring mutations and it was found that in like-to-like matings they bred true, that is to say, the kittens were exactly like their parents. At first they were confused with other longhaired cats with points, such as the Colourpoint (Himalayan) Persian, but they were proved to be true Siamese and were recognized in America in 1970.

Balinese cats have long, svelte bodies and wedge-shaped heads, with large, pointed ears and almond-shaped eyes. The long, flat-lying hair is fine and silky and there is no 'ruff' as in the Persian Longhair. This elegant cat was called the Balinese because it reminded breeders of Balinese dancers.

The CFA in America recognizes only the four basic Siamese point colours. Other point colours take the name Javanese. In Britain, all the point colours within the Siamese range are acknowledged.

FACT FILE

● The Balinese should have hair 5cm (2in) or more in length but does not have the ruff of fur around the neck that is usual in Persian Longhairs.

● The coat of the Balinese is very silky and non-matting making it easier to groom than other longhaired cats. However, daily grooming is necessary.

Below: *This attractive Balinese is a Red Tabby-point. It has a creamy white body colour and deep vivid blue eyes. It acquired its name because of its likeness in grace and agility to Balinese dancers.*

matings between Siamese cats and bi-coloured American Shorthairs. Like the Birman (see page 43), it has white paws. The forepaws are white only to the ankles, whereas the hind legs have white extending to the hocks. The coat pattern is Colourpoint (Himalayan) and the muzzle is white. The points are bi-coloured, and can be either seal and white or blue and white.

Because of its parentage, the Snowshoe, or 'Silver Laces' as it is sometimes called, has a heavier build and a rounder head than the Siamese. The eyes should be vivid blue and the nose has a break in the profile. The cat's temperament is quieter and less demanding than that of the Siamese. It is good natured and friendly. The Snowshoe is recognized by some US cat associations and has recently become known in the UK.

THE FOREIGN (ORIENTAL) SHORTHAIR

Known as the Foreign Shorthair in Britain and the Oriental Shorthair in the United States, this breed has the lithe graceful body of the Siamese, from which it has been bred. The standard requires the Foreign to be fine-boned with a long wedge-shaped head, straight profile and strong chin. The ears should be large and pointed, and the eyes almond-shaped. With its inquisitive nature, intelligence and boundless energy, this breed makes a delightful and affectionate pet.

In Britain, the Foreign Shorthairs are all solid coloured cats, and varieties include the White, Black, Blue, Lilac, Red and Cream. The brown is known as the Havana. Recent experimental varieties include the Cinnamon, Caramel, Apricot and Beige, although some of these colours cannot be reliably produced.

In the United States, the Oriental Shorthair comes in all these colours and many more — in fact, there are over 463 accepted shades and coat patterns, including the Tipped, Shaded, Smoke, Tortoiseshell, Tabby and Torbie (patched tabby).

The Foreign (Oriental) White Shorthair

This breed was developed in the 1960s and 1970s by mating white Domestic Shorthairs to Siamese cats. It is one of the most striking of the Foreigns, with a smooth white coat and pink nose leather and paw pads. In Britain, the almond-shaped eyes must be a clear, brilliant blue, whereas in America the eyes may be blue or green. Amber or odd eyes are not allowed. Unlike many other blue-eyed white cats, this breed is rarely deaf.

The Foreign Black (Oriental Ebony) Shorthair

With its jet black coat and emerald green eyes, this is a dramatic looking cat, known as the Foreign Black in Britain and the Oriental Ebony in the United States. It was only established as a breed in the 1970s when interest in it blossomed. Prior to this, it was bred experimentally or by chance and the cats were sold as pets rather than for showing. The coat should be raven black with no rustiness, the nose leather black and the paw pads black or brown.

The Foreign (Oriental) Lilac Shorthair

This delightful variety was developed in Britain in the 1960s during the Havana breeding programme. It has a pinkish-grey coat with a frosty grey tone. The nose leather and paw pads are lavender and the eyes a rich green.

THE HAVANA

The brown variety of Foreign Shorthair is known as the Havana in Britain. It resembles the Brown Oriental Shorthair of the United States rather than the Havana Brown.

Foreign Black
(Oriental Ebony)
Shorthair

Foreign (Oriental)
White Shorthair

Red-tipped
Oriental
Shorthair

FACT FILE

• The Havana often wears an expression which is both gentle and wistful; in competition, British judges call this the 'Havana look'.

• The Havana Brown mother cat often holds long conversations with her kittens.

• The Foreign (Oriental) Shorthair is curious and energetic but it is a great escapologist and may stray.

The Havana resulted from a breeding programme launched by two British breeders in the 1950s. The idea was to produce a mahogany-brown coloured cat of Siamese appearance. Another brown cat, the Burmese, had already begun to make an appearance in Europe but it was dark brown (sable) in colour. Developed from matings between Seal-point Siamese cats and other oriental type shorthairs, the Havana was so named because of its tobacco coloured coat. Despite criticism over its similarity to the Burmese, this breed was given official GCCF recognition in 1959 under the name of Chestnut Brown Foreign Shorthair. After this, it was further developed by matings with Siamese cats to create a more 'oriental' appearance. In 1970, the name was changed back to Havana.

The Havana has the same sleek body of the Siamese but without the colour restricted to the points. Unlike the Siamese, it has green eyes. Kittens are born a paler colour than the adult cat, and they may have faint tabby markings or white hairs but these gradually disappear.

Above: *The Foreign or Oriental White has a slender body and frosty white coat. Although it looks like a delicate china ornament, it is active, generally healthy and needs exercise.*

The Havana is an active and playful cat. It loves to hunt and play games and needs plenty of human companionship. Although intelligent and extroverted like the Siamese, it is a somewhat quieter cat than its relative.

THE HAVANA BROWN

This breed has the same origins as the British Havana but whereas the latter was bred back to Siamese to preserve its oriental type, the Havanas which arrived in the United States in the mid 1950s were never allowed to mate back to Siamese. Consequently, the Havana Brown, as it is known in the United States, is less 'oriental' in type, with a heavier build than its British relative.

The body of the Havana Brown is medium-sized and well muscled. The neck, legs and tail are medium in length. The breed has a more rounded head than the British Havana and the muzzle has a pronounced break on both sides behind the whisker pads. This makes the muzzle look almost square. The ears are large, tilt forwards and have rounded tips. The eyes are oval and the colour must be a vivid and even shade of green. A deeper shade of green is preferred.

These cats — the Havana, the Havana Brown and the Foreign (Oriental) Shorthairs — are active, intelligent and easy to groom, and appreciate human company. All have some Siamese blood but the Havana Brown has the least.

Havana

Foreign Lilac (Oriental) Shorthair

Havana Brown

THE EGYPTIAN MAU

The Ancient Egyptians called their cats Mau, which is the Egyptian word for cat. Depicted on a frieze in the ancient tombs in Thebes (c. 1400BC) is a spotted cat stalking duck with his master. This was the Egyptian Mau, the only natural breed of spotted domesticated cat. Centuries later, in the 1950s, spotted cats were seen to live in and around the Egyptian city of Cairo and it was presumed that the spotted cat of long ago and this later spotted cat were one and the same breed. Seen in a cat show in Rome by a Princess Troubetskoy who then took one home with her to the USA, these cats were said to look more cobby and slightly heavier than the Siamese.

In America, immediate interest was shown in the Egyptian Mau but it was 15 years before it was given official recognition. The CFF (Cat Fanciers Federation) recognized this breed in 1968 and the CFA recognized it in 1977. The CFA standard requires the Egyptian Mau to strike a good balance between the bulkiness of the cobby types and the sveltness of the oriental types.

The general impression of the Mau should be that of an active and muscular cat. The head should be gently rounded without the pronounced wedge of the Siamese. The ears are large and moderately pointed and the eyes large, almond-shaped and light green in colour. The hind legs are proportionately longer than the front so that the Mau looks as though it is on tip-toe when standing upright. The tail is medium-long in length and tapers at the tip.

The Egyptian Mau has a broken barred and spotted coat pattern. The coat of the Silver

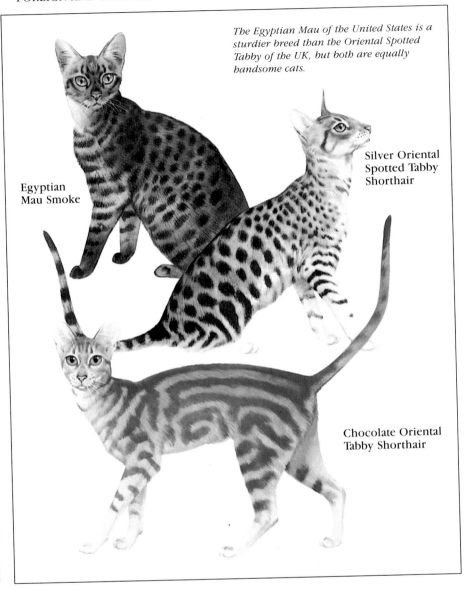

The Egyptian Mau of the United States is a sturdier breed than the Oriental Spotted Tabby of the UK, but both are equally handsome cats.

Egyptian Mau Smoke

Silver Oriental Spotted Tabby Shorthair

Chocolate Oriental Tabby Shorthair

Mau has a silver ground colour with charcoal markings. In addition to the Silver, the Mau is also accepted in Bronze and Smoke by the CFA. The Bronze is dark bronze shading to cream and the markings are dark brown. The Smoke Mau has a charcoal coat and black markings. All colours have black or dark brown paw pads and the Smoke Mau has black nose leather. Both the Silver and the Bronze Mau have brick red nose leathers. As the Egyptian Mau is a natural breed, the CFA does not allow inter-breeding with other breeds of cat.

THE ORIENTAL SPOTTED TABBY

While the Egyptian Mau was being bred in America, a British breeder, who was also fascinated by the Ancient Egyptian spotted tabby cat, decided to create her own breed. The breeding programme included matings between British Havanas and Siamese Tabby-points. At first, these cats were also known as Egyptian Maus but on application to the GCCF for breed recognition (given in 1978), the name was changed to Oriental Spotted Tabby.

The Oriental Spotted Tabby is of a more graceful, oriental type than its heavier American counterpart. The spotted coat pattern is the only pattern fully recognized in Britain. The breed may, however, be seen in 28 different colours and colour combinations! Ticked, classic and mackerel tabby coat patterns have also been developed. Oriental Tabbies have 'gooseberry' green eyes, except in the Red and Cream when copper through to green is permitted. All the Oriental Tabbies have lively personalities and demand lots of attention.

THE OCICAT

Completing the range of Oriental Tabbies is the Ocicat. This elegant spotted tabby cat was produced in the USA from matings between a Chocolate-point Siamese male and a half-Siamese, half-Abyssinian female. It was named the Ocicat because of its similarity in appearance to the Ocelot (see page 11). It is quite a large cat mainly known in dark and light chestnut. Twelve colours in all are accepted for competition in the USA. Leathers correspond to the coat colour and the eyes can be gold, copper or green.

Above: *The Silver Oriental Spotted Tabby has a clear silver ground colour with charcoal markings. The eyes are attractively ringed with black and are bright green. The tail has the characteristic tabby rings.*

Below: *As it rests in the leafy undergrowth, this sleek Chocolate Oriental Spotted Tabby looks very much like a wild cat with its half-closed eyes, ringed black-tipped tail and rich brown spotted tabby markings.*

with an ample chest, substantial bone structure and well-developed muscles. The round head has a blunt, wedge-shaped muzzle, and the round eyes are set wide apart as are the medium-sized ears. The strong legs have rounded paws. The British standard calls for a more elegant cat of a modified oriental type. In both the US and UK standards the coat should be fine and glossy, satin-like in texture and lying close to the body. This glossy coat is characteristic of all Burmese and indicates good health.

In the United States, the Brown Burmese is called the Sable. Other accepted varieties

Left: *A rich sable brown is the original coat colour of the Burmese and is the one that is typical of the breed. Pictured here is a Brown Burmese of excellent British standard.*

Below: *This Cream Burmese has the oriental type head which is so typical of the British standard. Shown here are the wide cheekbones, the short, blunt wedge-shaped muzzle and the slanted eyes.*

THE BURMESE

A brown oriental looking female cat called Wong Mau was imported from Rangoon to the United States in 1930. She arrived in the port of New Orleans in the company of a sailor and was then passed on to a Dr. Joseph L. Thompson who, fascinated by the richness of her coat colour, decided to show her and, later, to breed from her. However, since there were no males of Wong Mau's type available, she was mated to the next possibility which was a Siamese. The ensuing kittens were considered to be 'Siamese of poor type' and so crosses between the kittens and back to Wong Mau herself eventually produced the typical all-over sable brown Burmese which we know today.

Given CFA recognition in 1936, the breed was further developed by Dr. Thompson and other US breeders. This development involved some outcrossing to Siamese but, because this created too strong a Siamese look in the Burmese, the CFA suspended registration during the late forties and early fifties.

The first brown Burmese kittens came to Europe during the late 1940s. The Brown Burmese was given GCCF recognition in 1952 and the Blue in 1960. The breed is now extremely popular throughout Europe.

Official body standards for the Burmese differ in America from those in Britain. The US body shape should be medium-sized

in America are the Blue, Champagne (Chocolate) and Platinum (Lilac). In Britain, as a result of selective breeding, a wide range of coat colours is recognized for the Burmese. Varieties include the Brown, Blue, Chocolate, Lilac, Red, Cream, Brown Tortie, Blue Tortie, Chocolate Tortie and Lilac Tortie. The eye colour can be any shade of yellow, from chartreuse to amber, with golden yellow preferred. In the USA, the deepest yellow and gold are preferred.

In the adult Brown Burmese, the coat colour should be a rich, warm, seal-brown gradually shading to a lighter brown on the underparts. The ears and mask are darker. The Blue Burmese has a soft, silver grey coat, slightly darker on the back and tail. A distinct silver sheen should be seen on rounded areas

Right: *The Burmese are easy to groom and the Brown and Red Burmese show off their coats to perfection. Paler coats are also lovely, like this Lilac Tortie (Lilac-Cream) which is a more recent addition to the breed.*

FACT FILE

•In France, the Burmese is known as the Zibeline which means 'sable' — the colour of the fur.

•The Burmese is lively and friendly towards people, including strangers and children; it enjoys sleeping in human beds.

•The first variation from the normal colour of the Burmese cat was blue; this was so unexpected that the blue kitten was registered as 'Sealcoat Blue Surprise'.

Brown Burmese (USA)

Red Burmese

Lilac Tortie Burmese

such as the ears, face and paws. The Lilac (Platinum) Burmese has a delicate grey coat with pinkish undertones. The Chocolate (Champagne) Burmese has a coat the colour of milk chocolate, even-toned throughout. The ears and mask may be slightly darker. The coat colour of the Red Burmese is a light tangerine colour with slight tabby markings. Its ears should be slightly darker than the coat. The Cream Burmese has a rich cream coat with slightly darker ears. The nose leather and paw pads for each variety should correspond to the coat colours.

The Tortoiseshell colours were developed mainly in Britain. The Brown Tortie Burmese has a black and red tortoiseshell coat pattern and the Blue Tortie Burmese has a blue and cream tortie coat. The nose leather and paw pads for both should be, respectively: plain or blotched brown and pink, and plain or blotched blue and pink. There are also Chocolate and Lilac Torties.

Of all the breeds, the Burmese is probably one of the best suited for the family environment. With all the curiosity and intelligence of the Siamese, it has the advantage of being

much quieter and less destructive in nature than its relative. Burmese are affectionate cats, enjoying the company of people and liking nothing better than to join in with human activities. They are athletic, adventurous and have the reputation of being good hunters, courageously tackling quite large prey. Active, but without the highly-strung temperament of some oriental breeds, the Burmese enjoys playing games. The female makes a very good mother, often coming into season at the age of seven months and producing litters of five kittens.

Above: *The Korat's eyes are large and luminous, well-rounded when open and with an Asian slant when closed. Fully recognized in the USA, this quiet-natured cat has recently reached championship status in the UK.*

THE KORAT

In their native country of Thailand (Siam) the Korat was thought to bring good luck. Called the Si-Sawat (meaning good fortune), these cats were prized for their beauty. They most probably originated in Thailand's Korat province, although they are also known to have lived in other parts of that country.

Ancient manuscripts created by artists and writers in Ayudha, ancient capital city of Siam, tell of a blue cat having: 'Hairs so smooth, with roots like clouds and tips like silver' and 'eyes that shine like dewdrops on a lotus leaf'. These same manuscripts depict a blue cat with a heavy, cobby build. The fine blue coat with its silver tips remains to this day but in Britain the Korat is now medium-sized, muscular and semi-cobby in build. In the USA, however, the heavy cobby build has been maintained. The head of the Korat is heart-shaped and the nose is short with a gentle nose break. The eyes are green, and the nose leather and paw pads dark blue or lavender. The Korat was recognized in the USA in 1966 and in the UK in 1975.

The Korat is a sweet, gentle and quiet cat that loves to be petted. It best suits a calm environment as it dislikes sudden loud noises.

THE RUSSIAN BLUE

The Russian Blue is a natural breed, thought to have originated in the White Sea port of Archangel in northern Russia. Sailors brought it to Europe in the 1860s where it was known under several names: the Archangel Cat, the Maltese, the Spanish and the Russian. Less heavy and not as cobby as the British Blue of the time, the Russian's popularity waned by comparison to its British counterpart. But interest was revived in the 1950s when Siamese blood was introduced into the breed. This 'Siamese look' is now considered undesirable.

The Russian Blue first arrived in the United States in 1947 and the first Russian Blue club was formed in 1950. Only Blues are recognized for competition in the USA while the Blue, the White and the Black Russian are recognized in the UK.

The Russian Blue is a medium to large cat with a short dense coat. A medium blue colour is preferred in the United Kingdom, and a paler blue in the USA. The fur is a solid blue to its tips which are silver like those of the Korat. The head is wedge-shaped and the neck is covered with thick fur. The eyes should be almond-shaped, wide apart and green in colour.

The Korat and the Russian look similar in colour but do differ. The Korat has a fine, close-lying single coat while the Russian's double coat is soft and plush.

Korat

Russian Blue kitten

Russian Blue

THE TONKINESE

Developed in Canada and the USA in the 1960s and 1970s, the Tonkinese is a cross between the Burmese and the Siamese. It is a brown cat of oriental type, possessing the characteristics of both breeds from which it is derived. Tonkinese have a lively temperament and they love being with people; with the quiet, affectionate nature of the Burmese and the inquisitiveness of the Siamese, they make delightful pets

The Tonk, as it is sometimes known, was recognized first in Canada in 1974, then in the USA the following year. It has been seen in Britain but has not yet been accepted by the GCCF. It is a medium-sized cat with a slightly rounded wedge-shaped head. It has a squarish muzzle, round-tipped ears and almond-shaped, slightly slanting eyes. The tail tapers to a point and the slim legs have small dainty paws. The soft coat lies close to the body and the Siamese points merge into the body colour giving a darker mask, legs and tail. There are five different colour varieties: Natural Mink, Honey Mink, Champagne Mink, Blue Mink and Platinum Mink. The nose and paw leathers are respectively: brown, mid-brown, cinnamon-pink, blue-grey and pewter-grey. The eye colour should be blue-green.

THE BOMBAY

Like the Tonkinese, the Bombay is a Burmese hybrid. It has a fine, short coat which is satin-like in texture and dense black in colour. A Bombay kitten may have a 'rusty' coat at first but the coat will gradually become a dense black with age. The Bombay's eyes are gold to a deep copper colour.

Produced in the USA in 1958 of Sable Burmese and Black American Shorthair parents, the Bombay was, by 1976, accepted

Both the Tonkinese and the Bombay were derived from the Burmese cat. The Tonkinese had Siamese and Burmese parents and the Bombay had Shorthair and Burmese parents. So, both of these breeds have some of the Burmese temperament; they are affectionate and love human companionship.

Natural Mink Tonkinese

Champagne Mink Tonkinese kitten

Bombay

FACT FILE

• To keep the ancestry pure and to preserve the quality of the coat, it is forbidden to mate the Korat to any other breed.

• The coat of the Korat does not moult like that of other breeds; this makes grooming easy.

• The Tonkinese is bred only to other Tonkinese and the resulting litter produces 50% Tonkinese, 25% Siamese and 25% Burmese.

• The Bombay has been described as a 'mini black panther' with a patent leather coat and copper penny eyes.

for championship status. It has not yet been recognized in Britain.

The head is similar in shape to that of the Burmese and the face is full and tapers to a well-developed muzzle. The medium-sized body is muscular. The legs are in proportion to the body and tail, and are straight and medium in length. The nose leather and paw pads should be black and the deepest copper eye colour is preferred.

Playful and intelligent, the Bombay dislikes solitude and appreciates human companionship. It is active and good with children and other animals.

THE ABYSSINIAN

The Abyssinian has a 'ticked' (agouti) coat pattern and a likeness to the wild cat *Felis lybica*. It also looks very similar to pictures of Ancient Egyptian cats. It is possible to imagine that the Abyssinian is the direct descendent of these ancient cats. A more likely theory is that early breeders were influenced by the pictures and murals of the Egyptian cats and produced the Abyssinian from 'ticked' cats of oriental appearance.

A Mrs Barret Lennard brought a cat named Zula to Britain from Abyssinia (now Ethiopia) at the end of the Abyssinian War in 1868. Zula became the foundation for the British breeding programme. Consequently, this breed became known as the 'Abyssinian'. Its British listing in 1882 makes this lovely breed one of the oldest on record.

In 1909, the 'Aby' as it is affectionately called was exhibited in Boston, USA, and the breed was first recorded by the CFA in 1917. The Ruddy (called the Usual in the UK), the Red (called the Sorrel in the UK), the Blue and the Fawn are the four officially recognized varieties in the USA. The Usual, Sorrel and the Blue are fully recognized in Britain.

This active feline makes an ideal companion and prefers to be a 'special pet' rather than live in groups of its own kind. It is also gentle, playful and good with children.

Although very similar, the American and British body standards for the Abyssinian do differ slightly. The American standard calls for a slightly rounder head than the British, with a shorter, more moderately wedge-

Shown here are the Sorrel (Red) Abyssinian with its rich red brown coat and the Usual (Ruddy) with its apricot coloured coat. Also shown is the Singapura, a natural breed of 'ticked' cat from Singapore.

Singapura

Ruddy Abyssinian kitten

Sorrel (Red) Abyssinian

shaped face. The overall requirement in both countries is that the Abyssinian be a medium-sized cat of modified oriental type with a firm, lithe and muscular body. It should give an eager, athletic impression and show a lively interest in its surroundings. The British standard requires that the Abyssinian should not have a large or coarse build, and that any sign of cobbiness is a fault. The eyes should be almond-shaped, set wide apart, large and expressive. A squint is a fault. The ears should be large, wide-based and cupped as though listening and, preferably, tufted.

The 'Aby' is Siamese-like in shape, though not as long in the body as the Siamese. It is also Siamese-like in voice but much quieter. This cat does not display the fiery temperament of its supposed ancestor, the Egyptian cat, which, it was said, rode into battle on its master's back, springing on to the enemy with outstretched claws!

The coat of the Abyssinian is short, but long enough to accommodate two or, preferably, three bands of 'ticking'. The hair is fine, silky, and close-lying yet dense and springy to the touch. The original colour of

the breed was that of the Usual (Ruddy) which has ruddy orange or deep apricot base hair with black ticking. The Blue Abyssinian has cream ground hair shading to blue-grey with deep slate blue ticking.

Because the copper red colour of the Red (Sorrel) is not the same red as in the solid Red or the Red Tabby Shorthair, Britain and Canada decided to call the Abyssinian Red the Sorrel, to avoid confusion. This cat has a lustrous copper red coat with deep apricot base hair and chocolate ticking. Eye colour in the Abyssinian should be amber, hazel or green in the UK and gold or green in the USA.

In Britain there are also 25 other varieties which have only provisional recognition — that is, they have not yet reached championship status. These include the Lilac, Chocolate, Cream and Silver plus varieties with a tortoiseshell coat pattern.

THE SOMALI

When longhaired kittens appeared in shorthaired Abyssinian litters, breeders believed it was the result of a mutation (a sudden change in the 'make-up' of the individual).

Above: Resting in a typical 'wild cat' pose, this Sorrel (Red) Abyssinian shows off its firm, muscular body and its rich, copper red coat. The chocolate ticking shades into heavier markings on the face and tail.

The Somali is the longhaired version of the Abyssinian. Recognized in the Usual (Ruddy) and the Sorrel (Red) colours, it is only a matter of time before the entire range of Abyssinian coats are possible.

Ruddy Somali

It was soon discovered, however, that the ancestors of these cats had at one time been crossed with longhaired cats. This resulted in the occasional re-emergence of the longhair characteristic. In the 1950s and 1960s, breeding programmes produced the longhaired Abyssinian under the name of Somali. The first breed club was formed in 1972, with US and Canadian recognition following in 1977. The Somali is at the preliminary recognition stage in Britain.

This lovely cat, with its richly coloured medium-long hair, is seen in the Ruddy (Usual), the Red (Sorrel) and the Blue coat colours and is very popular in the USA, Canada, Europe and Australasia. The Somali has all of the Abyssinian characteristics, except in the voice which is very quiet.

THE SINGAPURA

The Singapura is a natural breed of cat which is native to Singapore. With its gold eyes and short ivory and brown 'ticked' coat, this little cat is similar to the Abyssinian in many ways except in head size and conformation. It is smaller than the average cat at around 4-6kg (9-13lb).

In its homeland, the free-ranging Singapura lived in the drains and was known as the 'drain cat'.

It can be found in many colours and coat patterns in Singapore but only the ivory and brown variety is exported. Recently imported into the USA, the Singapura was first shown there in 1976. Still quite a rare breed, it may now be seen in the UK.

Occasionally, a kitten bearing an unusual characteristic or feature is born into a litter of normal kittens. Sometimes this unusual characteristic is a throwback from earlier generations. For example, when a longhaired kitten is born to shorthaired parents, it is probably because many generations ago there was a longhaired cat in the family.

Alternatively, the new characteristic may be the result of a change in the kitten's 'genetic make-up'. The factors of inheritance, known as genes, are responsible for passing all characteristics of a living thing from one generation to another. Genes are what make kittens (or children for that matter) look like their parents. Sometimes these genes change their structure when they are being passed down from parent to offspring. A change in a gene's structure which results in a change in one of the offspring's characteristics is called a 'mutation'.

Each of the cats in this section has an unusual feature that sets it apart from other cat breeds. Some characteristics, such as the hairlessness of the Sphynx, the taillessness of the Manx, and the curly-coat of the Rex, are the result of mutations. The long hair of the Cymric, on the other hand, is the result of an 'old gene' — a throwback from past generations.

The Manx is of particular interest as it carries what is known as a 'lethal' gene. Most genes that control characteristics such as coat colour, coat pattern and body build are passed on from one generation to another with no harmful side-effects. The gene responsible for taillessness in the Manx, however, does have harmful side-effects. It causes abnormalities of the backbone, and, if a tailless Manx is mated to a tailless Manx, the unborn kittens die in the womb. To avoid fatality, tailless Manx have to be mated to

stumpies (very short tailed Manx) or, better still, to normal cats. The responsibility lies with the breeder to ensure that the cat is not disadvantaged by these genetic factors.

THE PEKE-FACED PERSIAN

The Peke-faced Persian was developed from solid Reds and Red Tabby Persians in the 1930s. It is recognized in North America and Canada but not in Britain.

This cat bears a close facial resemblance to the Pekingese dog from which it gets its name. It has a short, flattened nose and a high forehead with an indentation between the prominent eyes. The CFA states that the head should resemble as much as possible that of the Pekingese dog and that there should be an extremely wrinkled muzzle. The body should otherwise be the same as for all Persians Longhairs.

Above: *This American Peke-faced Persian is a magnificent specimen and many hours of grooming have resulted in this splendid fluffed-out coat. The solid Red is difficult to breed to perfection and almost impossible to produce without some tabby markings.*

Right: *This Ragdoll kitten is a Seal-point Bicolour. Behind the pile of logs, it hides a long, flowing tail — also seal coloured. Ragdoll kittens are born white and, since they mature slowly, it may be three years before the kitten's coat is fully developed.*

The 'peke-face' originally occured naturally and spontaneously. Breeders decided to selectively mate these peke-faced cats to accentuate the short pug nose and large, round eyes. As a result of this selective breeding, the Peke-faced Persian acquired some special problems. Blockages and distortions of the tear ducts often occur and the cat may have trouble breathing. Sometimes the teeth do not align properly so the cat may have feeding problems. The aim of the breeders has been to produce a cat with the required features but without these problems. However, the Peke-faced Persian has been the subject of much controversy because its extreme characteristics can be harmful to the health of the cat. To avoid problems, owners of a Peke-face should regularly cleanse the eyes and have the teeth inspected.

The Peke-faced Persian is bred in only two varieties. The self coloured Red is a deep rich red and the Red Tabby has a red ground colour with darker red markings in either the classic or mackerel tabby patterns. Both varieties should have brick red nose leathers and paw pads and copper eyes.

FACT FILE

•The Ragdoll is a gentle, quiet and dependent cat, well suited for apartment living.

•The Ragdoll is a heavy cat; males weigh around 6-9kg (15-20lb) and females weigh about 4-5kg (9-12lb).

•The Peke-faced Persian has been known in North America for half a century but the GCCF have not yet given it official status.

These sturdy looking Bi-colours, like all the Ragdolls, are calm, placid cats with quiet voices. The Peke-faced Persian shown here is a loyal and affectionate cat which requires much love and care.

Lilac-point Bi-colour Ragdoll kitten

Chocolate-point Bi-colour Ragdoll

Red Tabby Peke-faced Persian

THE RAGDOLL

The Ragdoll originated in California of mixed ancestry — supposedly a White Persian, a Birman and a non-pedigree Burmese. This cat is an unusual breed with two unique attributes. When picked up, it relaxes and goes limp like a rag doll — hence the name. Also, some Ragdolls allegedly have a high tolerance to pain. Both of these characteristics can render the cat vulnerable — especially if the cat lives in a house where there are other animals and boisterous children and where any injury may go unnoticed. In addition, the Ragdoll is said to be fearless with little sense of danger. Owners should be prepared to accept the extra responsibility of caring for a cat of this breed.

The first Ragdolls were a litter born to a White Persian queen who had been hurt in an accident. Some people thought that this had contributed to the unusual qualities found in the kittens. The results of physical injuries, however, cannot be passed on to offspring, so this theory, while intriguing, has little scientific merit. Tests show that there is no difference between the Ragdoll's body and the body of any other cat.

The Ragdoll is similar in appearance to the Birman, but it is larger and heavier in body with longer, thicker fur. It is bred in three coat patterns: the Colourpoint (Himalayan), the mitted (with white 'socks' and 'gloves') and the bi-colour. All three patterns may have any of the following point colours: seal, chocolate, blue or lilac. All these variations are recognized for competition in America. The cat itself is little known outside the United States at the present time.

THE SCOTTISH FOLD

In the early 1960s on a farm in Perthshire, Scotland, a shorthaired cat with folded ears named Susie had a litter of kittens. Two of these kittens also had ears which were folded forward, giving the appearance of a close fitting cap. The kittens became the foundation stock for the Scottish Fold breed.

A breeding programme in which Folds were mated to British Shorthairs and non-pedigree cats resulted in the Scottish Fold being shown at British cat shows. However, the fold of the ears, which can be at an angle of about 180°, was felt to be a deformity and damaging to the cat. The GCCF decided to cancel the Fold's registration.

Sometimes a deformity occured in which the legs and tail would become thickened. By careful breeding (mating the cat to other Shorthairs), the incidence of this deformity was reduced. Breeders exported the cat to America and several European countries. Now the Scottish Fold in the United States is a short, well-rounded cat with sturdy legs. It has a well-rounded head with a firm chin and large, round, wide-set eyes.

The Scottish Fold can have almost any colouring in the British and American Shorthair ranges. Generally the eyes are brilliant gold but, with some coat colours, they can be green, hazel or blue-green. The nose leather and paw pads should correspond to the coat colour. The Scottish Fold has a gentle disposition, is friendly, loves people and gets along well with other pets.

Below: This is a Black and White Bi-colour showing the typical Scottish Fold ears — it is also looking a bit startled, but this is due to its large, round eyes! The folded ears do not seem to cause any discomfort.

THE MANX

The tailless Manx cat comes from the Isle of Man, an island off the West Coast of Britain. In addition to being tailless, the Manx has longer hind legs than forelegs.

Tales of the Manx's origin are many. Some say that, in biblical times, the cat was the last creature to enter the Ark and an anxious Noah, slamming the door, chopped off its tail. Others say the Celtic raiders cut off the tails of the Isle of Man cats to decorate their helmets. To avoid distress to their kittens, mother cats began to bite the tails off first, until eventually the kittens were born without any tails. Nearer to the truth is that, in 1558, a ship from the Spanish Armada was shipwrecked on the Spanish Rock off the Isle of Man coast. Tailless cats on board swam ashore, becoming the forefathers of the present day Manx cat.

The Manx breed is known in three types: the completely tailless *rumpy,* the *stumpy,* with a 2.5-13cm (1-5in) tail (with approximately three vertebrae in the tail), and the *longie,* which has an almost normal tail.

Blue Tortoiseshell and White (Dilute Calico) Cymric

Blue Classic Tabby Scottish Fold kitten

Tortoiseshell and White (Calico) Scottish Fold

FACT FILE

●The Scottish Fold was not the very first cat of its type — drop-eared cats were known in China during the 18th Century and reappeared there in 1938. This means that cats with folded ears may have been around for over 200 years!

●The Japanese Bobtail is also known as the *maneki-neko* or 'welcoming cat' because it lifts one paw in greeting. Figurines of these cats can be seen in Japanese houses and shop windows in the 'beckoning' stance with one paw raised.

Red Tabby and White Manx

Black Manx kitten

Mi-ke Japanese Bobtail and kitten

Since its arrival in the USA in the 1930s, the Manx has been recognized by all American cat associations and has become quite popular. The breed should have a well-rounded appearance with a deep chest, a back which arches to a rounded rump, and sturdy forelegs with tall, hind legs. Complete taillessness (*rumpy*) is essential for competition. There should be a slight hollow in the rump where the tail ordinarily would have started. All colours and coat patterns are permitted in the UK. However, in the USA, chocolate, lavender, the Colourpoint coat pattern or any of these with white are not permitted for competition.

THE JAPANESE BOBTAIL

The Japanese Bobtail is centuries old. It is a natural breed of cat and the black, red and white tri-colour variety, called the *mi-ke*, is a symbol of good luck.

The breed's unique feature is the short tail which is held close to the body. The hair on the tail grows in all directions, making the tail look like a pom-pom. The Japanese Bobtail is slender with a soft, silky, medium-length coat and slanting eyes. The *mi-ke* is the most popular variety but this is, however, a female-only type. A wide range of other colours and coat patterns exists, although the Colourpoint (Himalayan) and the Abyssinian agouti patterns are not permitted.

In 1968, Bobtails were sent to the USA where the breed is now recognized. This breed is loyal, attractive and quietly vocal.

THE CYMRIC

In Canada in the 1960s, longhaired kittens appeared in shorthaired Manx litters, probably due to longhair ancestors. These longhaired tailless cats were developed into a separate breed which was recognized by the Canadian Cat Association (CCA) in the 1970s under the name of Cymric (coming from the Welsh word for Wales). Initially registered under the name Longhaired Manx, the Cymric is now accepted by all US cat associations. Except for its long coat, the Cymric is the same as the Manx in physique and temperament.

Left: Illustrated here are the tailless Manx from the Isle of Man, the Cymric — a longhaired tailless cat born to Manx parents, the Japanese Bobtail from Japan with its fluffy pom-pom tail and the Scottish Fold from Scotland with its uniquely folded ears.

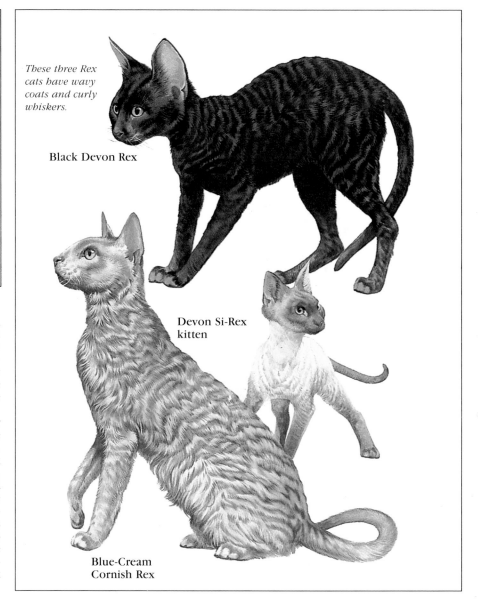

These three Rex cats have wavy coats and curly whiskers.

Black Devon Rex

Devon Si-Rex kitten

Blue-Cream Cornish Rex

THE CORNISH REX

In 1950, on a farm in Cornwall, England a farm cat produced a litter in which there was a curly-coated kitten. This male kitten named Kallibunker was mated back to his mother and several more curly-coated kittens were born. A breeding programme began and the new breed was named Rex.

In 1957, two descendants of Kallibunker went to the USA where they became the foundation of the Cornish Rex in America.

The GCCF standard for the Cornish Rex states that the breed should have a hard, muscular body with long, straight legs and small oval paws. The modified oriental type head should have a straight profile, oval-shaped eyes, large ears and curly eyebrows and whiskers. The short, plushy coat has no guard hairs (topcoat) and, in Britain, may be of any colour. In the USA, lavender, chocolate and the Colourpoint (Himalayan) coat pattern (see Si-Rex) are not recognized.

THE DEVON REX

In 1960, another curly-coated cat was discovered. Her name was Kirlee and she was born to a stray which lived in a disused tin mine in Devon, England. It was thought that this female was of the same type as the Cornish Rex, but this was found not to be true, and, in 1967, the Devon Rex and the Cornish Rex were recognized in Britain as separate breeds. In America, they were recognized by the CFA in 1979.

Unlike the Cornish Rex, the Devon has both undercoat and topcoat but the hair is coarser than in the Cornish. The Devon Rex has a muscular, medium-sized build and a rounded wedge-shaped head with a pixie-like face. Its whiskers and eyebrows are curly and the ears are large, sometimes tufted. In Britain, most colours are accepted other than any white markings (except in the Tortie and White) and bi-colours. Restrictions on colour for the Devon Rex in the USA are as for the Cornish Rex.

THE SI-REX

Matings between the Siamese and the Devon Rex or the Cornish Rex have resulted in Rex cats with a Colourpoint (Himalayan) coat pattern — that is, with the points of a Siamese. These cats, called Si-Rexes, resemble the type of Rex from which they are descended. In Britain, all the Colourpoint (Himalayan) coat colours are accepted. The eyes must always be blue. In the United States, the Si-Rex is not yet recognized.

With its wrinkled, sad-looking face, the Sphynx cannot claim to be the prettiest cat but it is said to be quiet and loving.

Sphynx

Above: *The wide-eyed, big-eared and curly-haired Devon Rex is particularly playful and mischievous. It is muscular, hardy and agile yet has a delicate appearance.*

Below: *Pictured here is a fine example of the distinctive, hairless Sphynx with its wrinkled forehead, huge bat-like ears, smooth skin and long, muscular body.*

THE SPHYNX

In Ontario, Canada, in 1966, a hairless male kitten appeared in a litter born to a black and white non-pedigree shorthair. From this mutant male was developed a hairless breed of cat officially called the Sphynx. It is also known as the Canadian Hairless, *Chat Sans Poils* (Cat Without Hair) and the Moon Cat.

The Sphynx is similar in appearance to the now extinct Mexican Hairless Cat which was thought to have descended from ancient Aztec hairless cats. It has a fine-boned and muscular ('chunky' by US standards) body, with long slim legs and a long thin tail. The head is neither wedge-shaped nor rounded and the ears are large. A fine velvet down covers the face and ears, being heaviest around the nose and mouth. The paws and tip of the tail are also covered in fine hair. Too much hair is considered a fault.

Because of its hairlessness, the Sphynx should be kept in a warm environment. Its skin feels smooth and hot to the touch (like warm suede) and should be sponged daily to remove any 'dander' caused by sweating. Special care should be taken to dry the skin gently and thoroughly after cleansing.

The Sphynx is rarely seen outside North America where it has been recognized by only a few associations. In some European countries, it is banned by cat associations.

INDEX